THE POSTWARRIORS

THE POSTWARRIORS

◆

BOOMERS AGING BADLY

Roy Wepner

iUniverse, Inc.

New York Lincoln Shanghai

THE POSTWARRIORS
BOOMERS AGING BADLY

iUniverse books may be ordered through booksellers or by contacting:

iUniverse
2021 Pine Lake Road, Suite 100
Lincoln, NE 68512
www.iuniverse.com
1-800-Authors (1-800-288-4677)

ISBN-13: 978-0-595-42540-2 (pbk)
ISBN-13: 978-0-595-86869-8 (ebk)
ISBN-10: 0-595-42540-2 (pbk)
ISBN-10: 0-595-86869-X (ebk)

Printed in the United States of America

To my favorite baby boomer in the whole wide world, my wife Shelley Wepner.

And because the likelihood of my having another book to dedicate is so miniscule, to my favorite children of boomers in the whole wide world, my daughters Meredith and Leslie.

Contents

Lifestyles Of The Aging And Quirky

Boomers Looking Backwards

Boomers @ Home

Food For Boomer Thought

Caution: Boomers At Work (Or Not)

The Boomer Body Politic

Culture, Boomer Style

ACKNOWLEDGMENTS

First, and assuming it isn't unseemly to mention in the Acknowledgments the same people who appear in a Dedication, I would like to thank my wife Shelley and my daughters Leslie and Meredith. In addition to encouraging this project from the very beginning and helping me come up with ideas for the essays that led to this book, they were often among the precious few people who (I was reasonably certain) had actually read the finished products.

I am also most grateful to my oldest friend, Daniel Kornstein, a prolific and provocative writer in his own right. I drafted him as my writing coach, and he has been there with feedback, suggestions, and encouragement whenever I needed them. He makes an appearance at the end of Chapter 8.

I am hugely indebted to Michael Redmond, the Lifestyle Editor of the *Princeton Packet*. At a time when I had written only a few of these essays, he took a shot and began to publish them. This proved to be the beginning of an education for me, as I learned that some of the essays I had the most fun writing nonetheless did not meet Michael's standards regarding what was best for his readers. Hopefully, you will disagree with Michael as to the previously unpublished essays that appear in this collection. Even more importantly, whenever Michael favored me by publishing one of my columns, it would jolt me out of my complacency and stir up whatever creative juices I might have, just so I could replenish the supply of unpublished columns in Michael's in-box.

Last but by no means least, I thank my assistant Denise Ghilino, for converting my chicken scratchings into legible text and for patiently helping me nudge each piece upward or downward to just the right length. As you will notice in chapter 29, what passes for inspiration invariably hits me at a time and place where all I have handy are a legal pad, a pen, and the handwriting skills of a six-year-old.

INTRODUCTION

Remember when every baby boomer was going through a mid-life crisis?

I suppose this was mine. And I suppose it came a tad late.

Fast sports cars never really appealed to me, perhaps because I would need a very large shoehorn to insert myself into the driver's seat. Extramarital affairs were not my cup of tea either. I guess I considered myself lucky to have horn-swoggled one great woman into marrying me, and if she was crazy enough to stick with me, I wasn't quite dumb enough to screw up that particular good thing. Scrap my career and become a carpenter? Nah. I actually was enjoying practicing patent law and the company of my law partners. How dull is *that*?

But as I approached my 40s in the late 1980s, I started to feel like I needed to break out of my routine just a wee bit. Holding on to my day job, I tried teaching for a time, doing gigs at two law schools. I liked it—really, I did—but after teaching two courses three times each, I found that the post-boomer expression "been there, done that" had begun to creep into my lexicon.

So I began to think about writing. Or, I should say, I began to revisit old thoughts about writing. I had actually done a bit of writing in high school. But then I studied engineering in college, and my interest in writing atrophied for quite some time.

When I became a lawyer, I started writing nonstop for a decade, then another decade, and then one more. Of course, most of what I wrote was stuff that no one in his or her right mind would choose to read: briefs, letters, pleadings, and the occasional stupefying patent application. Sure, every now and then I put pen to paper about something outside my legal practice, but it never amounted to much.

Around the time I turned 55, it occurred to me that if I was still planning to have a serious midlife crisis, I would now be forced to live to 110. I also came to the realization that the chances of my writing the Great American Novel—or, for that matter, any novel at all—were rapidly descending from slim toward none and perhaps beyond. *Oh wait!* Did I forget to mention this little pipe dream? I guess I assumed that you had figured out yourself that this is one more guy who thinks he can write—another lawyer, no less!—and would be on the *New York Times* Bestseller List if only he had the time to exhale that novel. What I *did* conclude was that a full-blown novel was just too much for me to take on. The sheer magnitude of the task was scaring me away from even getting started.

So I convinced myself that if I was ever going to write anything, it would have to happen in bite-size pieces—say 700 words a pop. I could do that, or so I thought. So I hatched this scheme to write a column of some sort for a publication of some ilk.

But what would this column be about? I had always heard it said that you need to write about what you know. Well, I knew something about patent law, but who would want to read it?

Of course, by the time I turned 55, I started to know something about getting older. Contrary to everything I and most baby boomers had assumed for so long, we were no longer America's precious youth. On the contrary, our generation was well on its way to becoming the most annoying irritant in history.

It occurred to me that much of what can be said about aging is pretty self-evident, needs no introduction, and can be awfully depressing. The actuarial realities do not change a whole lot from generation to generation.

But I also began to realize that much of the aging experience was actually somewhat humorous, if not altogether farcical. So I thought I could write a series of 700-word columns about the sometimes bitter, sometimes sweet, sometimes bittersweet experiences of aging, seen through the lens of the notorious baby boom generation.

To be sure, I harbor no illusion that my own experiences typify those of this vast generation. To begin with, strictly speaking, the baby boom generation encompasses people born over an entire 20-year period beginning at the end of World War II. I was born in 1947, as part of the leading edge of the baby boom, and I suspect that my experiences have differed greatly from those boomers who are, say, 15 years younger than I am.

I have also been far luckier than most boomers, and most people. So the essays I was going to write were from this perspective: someone who had dodged many of the bullets of misfortune that have wounded or felled many people in our generation.

Overcoming writer's block enough to generate a dozen potential columns, I still needed an outlet. Once again, luck was with me. At the time I started this project, I was living near Princeton, and had become familiar with a local newspaper known as the *Princeton Packet*. Princeton is a unique community, and the *Packet* is pretty special as local newspapers go. The *Packet* began to run my columns whenever it had the space and whenever one of my columns struck the editor's fancy. And although circumstances required me to relocate out of the

Princeton area, my luck continued, and the *Packet* remained willing to continue publishing my columns.

So after about three years of replenishing the supply of unpublished columns, I arrived at what I thought was a sufficient number of essays to put into a book—a rather small book, but a book nonetheless.

To my fellow early boomers who read this, I hope you will see some of your own experiences in these essays. And for those of you who are younger or older, perhaps this book will help you understand why it is that you have found our generation to be so irritating all these years.

Meet The Postwarriors

1

PEACE IN OUR TIME

For the aging but still enormous generation that was born beginning in the late 1940s—the generation that came to be known as the baby boomers once it became clear that calling it the "postwar" generation didn't do justice to its enormity—the war is over.

No, not "the war" which we baby boomers grew up hearing about through the '50s and '60s. The "big one" our parents lived through—or didn't. The one fought in Europe and the Pacific. The one they called Dubya-Dubya-Two even before baby boomer "Dubya" was born. For our parents' generation, it was the all-purpose frame of reference: all events large and small occurred before, during or after "the war."

No, for our generation, the war which is finally over is our personal war. The struggle to get educated, get a job, climb the ladder, and perhaps eke out some success—all while competing with the huge demographic bulge that was and is our baby boom generation.

Earlier and later generations love to say that we boomers had life handed to us on a silver platter. But as we look back on our past (a stretch of time that now seems to be—because it is—much longer than our future), I can't help thinking that our generation's motto should be this: nothing's ever easy.

Remember when we were teenagers looking for jobs after school or during vacations? It was never all that simple, because whenever a job opened up, there were baby boomers aplenty competing with us for the same job.

And remember the group of colleges that so comfortably accommodated prior generations? College became for us a battleground, where we fought with SAT scores and high school averages for suddenly scarce spaces. For every aspiring doctor, manager, entrepreneur or whatever in our generation, there were always others fighting for the same spot in medical school, the same promotion to middle management, or the same piece of market share. We won some battles, we lost some too, and—as we are reminded when we see homeless people our age—we took some casualties.

But for most of us, those wars are now largely over. If we haven't achieved our big dreams from the '60s, '70s and '80s, it probably isn't going to happen at all. Whoever we were destined to become, we are probably that person today. While a few of us still have mountains to climb, and fewer still will actually climb them, most of us are adjusting to the view we see today out of our office and home windows. For better or for worse, each of us boomers is now pretty much a done deal.

Yet a funny thing is happening as we gingerly work our way over the hump and come to terms with what we accomplished and what we didn't. Our children and our nieces and nephews—of the baby "boomlet" or "echo" generation—have now entered the trenches of their own personal battles. Some of their battlegrounds—like dot.com start-ups and women's sports leagues—do not even appear on our outdated maps. Their weapons of choice—Treos, Blackberries, PDAs—are a mystery to many of us. But they, like us, will go through good times and bad; they will win a few, and they will lose a few.

And while we are no longer the combatants, their wars feel like our wars, too. We may advise them, we may photograph and chronicle their victories, or we may just say I told you so. But because they are our kids, we still feel that thrill of victory and the agony of defeat. We may brag about our kids in a continuing game of one-upmanship, or we may blame them for things we didn't achieve.

But the reality is this: it's not so much about us any more. More and more, it's about them. Their wars are theirs. But for boomers who live through their children—either because we vainly see our kids as extensions of ourselves, or because we never quite won that last battle—we see their wars as our wars too.

All of which suggests that, for us "postwarriors" of the postwar generation, peace in our time may be an elusive dream.

The Body Boomer

2

EASY GUM, EASY GO

For some baby boomers, the moment occurred when we glanced down at our watches and discovered that the date (if not the time) had forever disappeared into the mists of presbyopia. And when we called over to ask a fellow boomer what the date was, she didn't hear us; or, if she did, she gave us the date but couldn't remember the month.

For other members of our generation, it was that epiphanic moment when we realized that our aching backs had allowed us to forget, for a few blissful moments, that our feet were killing us.

For certain baby boomers of the male persuasion, it was the day we discovered that our personal hydraulic systems—the ones which had allowed us to write our names in snow (in script!) back in the Eisenhower administration, and with which we melted buckets of cracked ice in those old porcelain urinals—were now barely adequate to propel a few lousy drops over the near edge of the bowl.

For our female counterparts, it may have been the day the internal thermostat went haywire: when the body got warm, it cranked up the heat.

For me, I think it was the day I settled into the chair for my first visit to a periodontist. As the hygienist breezed into the room, tools glistening, she cheerfully greeted me, "Welcome to the major leagues!" Easy gum, easy go.

The moment comes at different times for different members of our generation. But it does come for nearly all of us: the moment we realize that our bodies are nickeling and diming us to death.

It is said that our bodies start deteriorating the day we are born. Perhaps that is so, but who even noticed back then? We spent two or three decades feeling physically (if not emotionally) indestructible. There was little we couldn't do, and almost nothing we wouldn't at least try.

In hindsight, if we look carefully—which will probably require that we put on our glasses—we can see that certain events which seemed so insignificant back then were signs of things to come.

Maybe we should have taken a hint on those nights in college back in the '60s, when we punished our digestive systems with a witch's brew of cheap beer and greasy pre-McDonald's junk food, discovering that our stomachs were made not of cast iron, but only a thin sheet of tin foil.

Or perhaps we can see previews of aches and pains to come in the '70s and '80s, when we followed our children into sports we hadn't played in ages, only to come home to desperately burrow through drawers looking for ice packs, BEN GAY and ACE bandages. I can dimly recall the time I followed my kids onto the roller skating rink and discovered that while I still remembered how to *skate* after a 30-year layoff, I didn't quite recall how one was supposed to *stop*.

And remember those pounds we put on when we were in our forties? You know—the ones we knew we could shed whenever we wanted, like we always had before. Should we have seen trouble on the way when our relationships with those pounds began lasting longer than some of our marriages?

There is evidence of our creeping decrepitude everywhere. We see it in the growing number of pills we pop daily. We see it in the ever-increasing number of medical professionals we find in our lives (who even knew what a podiatrist did back in our heyday?). And we see it in the time we spend in front of a mirror, looking for hair in all the wrong places.

But appreciating that we are falling apart little by little leads to another realization: how lucky we are that we still can talk about these minor maladies and maybe even get a chuckle out of them. There are now plenty of baby boomers for whom a little gum disease or aching feet would seem like a stroll in the park, and those numbers are inexorably heading north. And as we reconnect with people at our high school and college reunions, we are reminded that there are those who (like us) had once idly daydreamed about crossing into the new millennium—but didn't.

3

GOD'S GIFT TO GASTROENTEROLOGISTS

For decades, gastroenterologists—the doctors who preside over our intestines and stomachs—toiled in relative obscurity. To outsiders, their field seemed just slightly north of urology, just slightly more pleasant to contemplate than proctology, and just slightly more pronounceable than otorhinolaryngology.

But a funny thing happened to gastroenterologists as the 20th Century slid into the 21st—actually two things. One was the rise to prominence of the colonoscopy. By now, we all know what it is: a procedure that explores our intestinal tracts, looking for polyps and other problems. By the late 1990s, the colonoscopy came to be seen as a procedure that was safe and so effective in spotting certain problems early that medical insurers saw the procedure as such a good hedge against future, more significant expenditures that they actually agreed to pay for it. A few well-publicized deaths from problems that an early colonoscopy might have detected raised everyone's consciousness about the procedure. And so, around the turn of the millennium, it came to pass that conventional medical wisdom dictated that everyone should have a colonoscopy after they turn 50.

As luck would have it, right about this time, a huge number of people started to turn 50—a veritable tidal wave known as the baby boom generation. And so began, in the offices of America's once obscure gastroenterologists, an endless parade of boomers armed with medical insurance and—in many cases—a decades-long fetish about fitness, health and "wellness,' all anxious to have instruments snaking around their innards looking for early signs of disease. While not long ago most boomers had no clue what a gastroenterologist was, today every self-respecting boomer "has" a gastroenterologist. And boomers have become God's gift to gastroenterologists.

Not surprisingly, all these colonoscopies have enriched our culture immeasurably. Today, when boomers gather, they share war stories about their colonoscopies. Of course, when you listen carefully, you quickly realize that these boomers aren't talking about the actual procedure. As anyone who has had the procedure will tell you, there's nothing to it. In most cases, the patients are put out just long enough and just deeply enough for them to have no idea that the procedure has come and gone. Nor (in most cases) are they talking about the results, which usually and happily prove to be negative.

No, these boomers—these courageous, daredevil, risk-taking scamps—are talking about the *preparation* for the colonoscopy: the evening (or, for some, the entire day) before the procedure, when we have to completely empty out our intestinal tracts. The methods vary from little pills to big jugs of foul-tasting potions. But the results are the same: the runs—lots of them—for hour after hour. Explosions, followed by a brief respite, followed by another beeline to the can, to the point that the fluffiest toilet paper feels like sandpaper.

Just listen to those boomers! You would think that after being too young for Korea, too disapproving and/or too cowardly for Vietnam, and too old for Desert Storm, boomers had finally found a true test of their physical and emotional mettle: a full night, or—for some overachievers—maybe even a full day of self-inflicted trips to the bathroom.

There is just a little bit of irony here. It has been said that no generation has had as much to say as the boomers. We have something to say about everyone and everything, and we say it incessantly. Show me a boomer, and I'll show you a talking head waiting to be discovered. We talk about our health more than even the early-bird-special gang in Florida. If we run out of people to talk to, we hit the chat lines on the internet, and talk to hundreds of strangers at a time. And on those rare occasions when we run out of things to say, we run to our shrinks and talk about *that*.

So forgive me for getting just a little chuckle out of this spectacle of the early 21st Century: the generation that practically invented diarrhea of the mouth has now given itself the real thing.

4

TAKE TWO AND CALL ME IN THE MORNING

To hear the pharmaceutical industry in the United States talk, you would think the industry is in the throes of death.

After all, Americans are traipsing to Canada to buy their drugs at lower prices. Cities and states, which pay for huge quantities of drugs, are trying to do the same. Third world countries fighting AIDS and the like are demanding access to American drugs, but can't afford the prices that the drug companies charge us and our insurers. And that perpetual irritant, the generic drug industry, is forever raising a ruckus about "Big Pharma" manipulating and abusing the patent system.

But I suspect that every day, at every drug company, there is a moment of prayer (or, for non-religious types, perhaps just silent contemplation) in which thanks are given for the ultimate savior, which will bring unimaginable riches to the drug industry for decades to come. It is bigger than any blockbuster drug, creating more titillation than even VIAGRA.

It is *us*, the baby boom generation.

Like a few million PACMAN characters, our oversized generation has consumed everything in its path, from vinyl records to college educations to lattes and sushi.

Now, we are consuming drugs. Big time. Tens of millions of boomers suffering the ravages of middle age and beyond, and taking drugs to fix those problems at every turn.

Have you noticed how our roster of doctors expands from year to year? As body parts deteriorate, we may enlist a cardiologist, a gastroenterologist, a dermatologist, and "ologists" we never even heard of. And chances are, for each doctor we see, we pick up a new drug or two. And lots of these drugs aren't like antibiotics, which you take for ten days and then you're done. No, it seems like for more and more of the drugs we take, we have a life sentence. So long as we want to keep our cholesterol down, or keep that little old prostate small, we have to keep popping those pills. Every day. Forever. (Gee, I wonder if the drug companies ever though about this.)

This has caused all sorts of problems. (I won't even talk about the expense; I'll leave *that* to the politicians.) For example, who can remember to take all this stuff every day? I take three prescription drugs a day, two in the morning and one at night. Can they really expect someone my age, who is hemorrhaging memory at an alarming rate, to remember to take his meds twice a day?

And then there's the little problem of my three "scrips" all running out at different times. If you run out of one, you can't wait until a second drug is due for renewal a week or two later. And your pharmacist won't let you renew the second one early, out of fear that we'll double dip. So now I seem to visit my local drug-store as often as I hit the dry cleaner.

Of course, the baby boom generation is no stranger to drugs. As a kid in the '50s, I sometimes thought I would explode from all the penicillin pumped into me.

By the '60s, "drugs" had taken on a new meaning for boomers. Many of us "experimented" with "recreational" drugs such as marijuana and LSD. Fortuitously, the only lasting damage done to many boomers was a slight and highly specific loss of memory: the ability to accurately answer the question, "Mom, did you do drugs back in the '60s?"

Today, drugs are still a source of recreation. But because the drugs come from some "ethical" drug company rather than some shady guy in a back alley, they are socially acceptable. We can pop a pill to give us renewed sexual potency, so long as a Fortune 500 company gets a little action too. I've even heard of doctors who prescribe LIPITOR for each other, just so they can eat red meat without concern.

Imagine! Pop a couple of pills on a Saturday night, and you can enjoy a guilty-free sirloin steak and maybe even a successful roll in the hay. I guess this is what they *really* meant when they used to talk about "better living through chemistry...."

5

WEIGHT FOR ME

For some time, it seemed like everyone you met who had a weight problem—which is to say, almost everyone you met—was on the "Atkins," "South Beach" or some other low-carbohydrate diet. We were treated daily to tales of hunger-free people losing copious amounts of weight, seemingly overnight.

But for this boomer, and perhaps others who have been around the weight loss track for a few decades, there was only one reaction to this exciting new 21st century phenomenon:

Yawn.

I for one did a low-carb gig in 1971. A friend of mine from work turned me on to a diet book entitled (I think) "Martinis and Whipped Cream." You could eat all the protein and fat you wanted, so long as you limited your daily intake of "carbocals" to some preset number.

Now remember, this was before anyone talked about cholesterol. And, in 1971, this boomer was only 24 and hadn't yet discovered that his body was not indestructible. So I started each day with eggs—yes, two (or maybe it was three) eggs every day for breakfast. And since I was a bachelor with a limited cooking repertoire, for dinner each night I made myself steak, with a side order of steak. And while I wasn't a big fan of martinis, I took my whipped cream "straight"—that is, straight from the REDDI-WHIP aerosol can to my uvula. Since the office in which we worked had a doctor's scale, my friend and I weighed in each weekday and dutifully recorded our progress on an improvised chart.

Yes, I lost weight on the "Martinis and Whipped Cream" diet. Actually, I lost *a lot* of weight (even after my buddy and I, having both lost 50 pounds, celebrated by eating *two* ribs-and-fries dinners *each*, and washing them down with hot fudge sundaes.) And the experience of this diet made such a favorable and lasting impression on me that I lost the same weight (no, not the same *amount* of weight, the very same weight) every year or two for three decades thereafter.

I even did a couple of tours of duty with Weight Watchers. I liked their diet: lots of fruit and starches; and the male chauvinist in me even got a secret pleasure out of being allowed to eat more than the women. Even showing up for the weekly weigh-in was cool those first few weeks, when those last few pounds I had gained—the ones with neither tenure nor seniority—quickly melted away. And since I was much bigger than my mostly female compatriots, my initial weight loss was truly impressive.

But when the backslide began—and it always did—I went AWOL, pretending (but only for a short while) that my 20-year-old bathroom scale, which could be persuaded to read just about any number, was just as accurate as the Weight Watchers scale. After that, I was MIA until the next post-New Year's amnesty period.

Yes, we boomers have seen lots of diets and weight loss gimmicks come and go over the years. Remember the grapefruit diet? And remember METRECAL? For me, they all work—until they don't. My doctor got it right one time when, after bemoaning my cholesterol, blood sugar and other levels, he described me as the kind of person who is capable of tremendous feats of willpower for spectacularly short periods of time.

Those boomers who, like me, have always had weight "issues" now face a certain amount of conflict as we pass through middle age, heading toward the indescribable next stage of life. On the one hand, our doctors tell us that being overweight increases our health risks. On the other hand, at our age, we're at the point that no one expects us to look as good as we once did.

No discussion of weight and diet would be complete without mentioning those boomers who have never been overweight, never obsessed about food, and even created well-adjusted children who never had food or weight problems. You are my idols and my role models. For this half-century of accomplishment, I salute you.

All seven of you.

6

MEDICINE: SOMETHING OLD, SOMETHING NEW ...

I get my annual physical about every 14 months. Yes, I know that means that my check-ups aren't exactly annual, and that there may be years in which I don't get a physical at all. What happens is that whenever I realize it's been a year since my last physical, I call my doctor's office to set one up. But I schedule it about two months down the road, so I have time to maybe lose enough weight to avoid the inevitable scolding from my doctor.

Scoldings aside, I actually like my doctor. He's a fellow boomer whose kids knew mine, so we always catch up a bit before we get down to business. And, of course, I have to plead *nolo contendere* to his scoldings.

Thus, when I called up recently to set up my every-14-months physical, I was surprised and concerned to hear that my doctor was himself on medical leave. However, I was assured that another doctor in the office was filling in and could give me the physical (after my obligatory crash diet, of course). Figuring that it might well be a good idea to have a second doctor get familiar with my aging carcass, I readily agreed. Of course, I pretended that my schedule was booked solid for two months but that I could squeeze it in shortly thereafter.

When the day for my physical rolled around (by which time I had lost a pathetically small amount of weight), I appeared at the doctors' office at the appointed time, and listened to the usual itemization of all the things my insurance *doesn't* cover. Once I was inside the examination room, a nurse measured my height (not yet decreasing, to my surprise) and weight (decreasing imperceptibly, but only after an alarming gain), and I waited to meet the new doctor.

I should not have been surprised to discover that the new doctor was female. After all, this being the 21st century, drawing a female doctor today is about as unusual as flipping a coin and having it land on heads.

What *did* throw me a bit was that the new doctor was young enough to be my daughter.

My first thought was about all the years of experience this doctor *didn't* have, as compared to my regular doc. My old doctor has probably handled hundreds of patients like me who wreak havoc on their metabolic systems, except during the run-up to their annual physicals, when they eat sensibly for a few days and hope to scam the HDL and LDL counters. With the new doctor, who knows? What if I was the first?

But as the exam progressed, and as the new doctor showed every indication of knowing exactly what she was doing, it got me thinking. Medicine has changed an awful lot since my old boomer doctor graduated from medical school. Had cholesterol even been invented then? My new doctor had the benefit of the latest medical thinking when she was trained, and she hasn't had enough time to forget it yet.

And perhaps there is something to be said for the extra objectivity a new doctor brings to her practice, particularly one who *hasn't* heard all of our excuses for not being constantly vigilant about health issues.

But there is one more reason we boomers should happily let those young doctors examine us. By helping them get the experience they need, they will morph into the old pros who—in a few years—will breeze into examination rooms and immediately instill complete confidence.

I certainly wish my old doctor a speedy recovery. And when he's back on his feet, I'll still be his patient. But I'm hoping that when he retires, I'll still be around, and I'll probably need a good doctor then more than ever. And in all likelihood, other boomer doctors who may still be practicing won't be taking on too many new patients.

And so when it comes to making the acquaintance of a doctor who is young enough to call you Mom or Dad, and who *wasn't* present at Woodstock, and who *never* saw the Mets play at the Polo Grounds, I say this:

No time like the present.

Boomers, Other Boomers, and Others

7

OLD CHILDREN, YOUNG CHILDREN, GRANDCHILDREN

"No, Billy, you can't go out tonight. You have to stay home and take care of little Uncle Joey and Aunt Jenny."

What baby boomer uttered *those* words? Children older than their own aunts and uncles? How did our generation manage to make *that* happen?

You could say that it was the inevitable result of two signature "freedoms" espoused by our generation: the freedom to change spouses as easily as we roll over our 401(k)s, and the freedom to procreate (with or without spouses) at any time from late adolescence to the week before menopause.

Our generation came of age during a period whose end points now seem to have been a century apart. It began in the 1950s—a period which actually started when Dwight D. Eisenhower was elected president in 1952, and lasted until the death of John F. Kennedy in 1963. The second phase of our coming of age was in the '60s, which really began the moment Lyndon Johnson stepped on Air Force One in Dallas in November 1963, and ended when Richard Nixon took his helicopter ride out of office in 1974. The notorious 1960s: jarring new music from long-haired druggies; rebellion; free love; Viet Nam; and—lest we forget—"finding ourselves."

Some baby boomers followed the lead of our parents and the traditions of the '50s. They married early, quickly had 2.4 children, bought a house in the suburbs, and lived like millions of Ozzies and Harriets. They're easy to spot now: they're the ones who are already grandparents. At the other end of the continuum are those of us who did their thing in the Peace Corps or wherever, eschewed commitments, and finally settled down to have children just as their biological clocks were winding down. Thus, you can visit a first grade class today and find the children of some baby boomers sitting next to the grandchildren of others.

Figuring out how this happened is easy. What's not so easy is figuring which group of boomers we should envy.

Those who became parents later in life began the adventure with more patience and more money. But as their children become adolescents—and we're using the future tense deliberately here—they may run out of steam just a little too soon. Those 401(k)s that were supposed to finance retirement may get rolled over into tuition payments.

Those who entered parenthood early had only youth, energy and maybe a used copy of Dr. Spock. But those children born between the late '60s and the mid-'70s had something which many children born in the late '80s and '90s of baby boomer parents might not have at all: grandparents.

Life in the 21st Century would be confusing enough if all we had was a spreading out of our children's generation. But it is complicated by a trend which our generation didn't start but which we took to the next level: divorce, second marriages and beyond. We even invented the prepackaged divorce: prenuptial agreements which spelled out all terms of a future split except for the actual date.

So we now have situations like this. Early boomers Harry and Eleanor, both born in 1947, marry in 1968. They have Susie in 1969, but the marriage goes downhill, and they divorce in 1979. In 1989, early boomer Harry marries late boomer (and late bloomer) Linda, who was born in 1955; and just before Linda's biological clock takes its last tick, Harry and Linda have Joey in 1999 and Jenny in 2001. Meanwhile, Susie—remember her?—was so messed up by her parents' bad marriage that she has a child out of wedlock in 1988 at the age of 19. This was Billy, the first grandchild of Harry and Eleanor. Eleanor had moved to Vermont after splitting up with Harry, so Susie and her son Billy move in with Harry and Linda.

And so it comes to pass that Harry and Linda have to go out, while Susie has to work late. And so Billy, now a teenager, gets to chase around that cute little toddler—his Aunt Jenny—and change the diapers of his little Uncle Joey.

And you wonder why neither our parents nor our children understand the baby boom generation.

8

WOMB TO TOMB

For much of the baby boom generation, the first big movie of our adolescence was "West Side Story," a musical about warring teenage gangs in New York City. Early in the film, we meet Riff, the leader of the Jets, and Tony, who has outgrown the Jets but still thinks of Riff as a brother. Despite their growing differences, they pledge each other to life-long friendship—as they put it, "womb to tomb."

Well, they did remain friends for life, but perhaps only because their lives turned out to be so short: Riff was stabbed by Bernardo a few scenes later at the rumble, and Tony was shot by Chino in the final scene. Womb to tomb in less than two decades.

Most baby boomers have now outlived Riff and Tony by a wide margin. But only a fortunate few of us have friends that go back so far into our past, and who are likely to be our friends for our remaining days, that they can truly be termed life-long friends.

If we're lucky, we started making friends in elementary school. As we progressed through other schools, jobs, the military, marriage, parenthood, new neighborhoods and what have you, we made new friends—again, if we were lucky.

Most friends we made along the way eventually fell by the wayside. But a select few did not, and these are the ones we salute today.

To be sure, it isn't easy to keep a friendship going over several decades. The reasons we lose friends are countless: geography (one or both people relocate); incompatible spouses or partners; the success of one leading to the jealousy of the other; misunderstandings that fester and grow; to name just a few.

But the friendships that last transcend all those issues and survive for decade after decade. The pal who drifted away for a few years because he didn't like your wife may come back into your life to help you through a rough (but, in your pal's view, overdue) divorce. The friend you lost touch with when she moved to the opposite coast may be the one who helps you adjust when an unwanted job trans-fer moves you into her territory.

It takes time and effort to nurture old friendships. After all, if we were lucky enough to make friends when we were young, we probably continued to make friends as we progressed into and through middle age. Our family and job responsibilities occupy so much of our time, and what with social commitments with our current friends, who has time to call that old fraternity brother, or the gal who sat in the next cubicle at your first job, or the old "summer" friend who went to your camp or vacationed every year at the same place your family did? After all, how much do you still have in common?

Not much, but that's just the point. Because the basis of the relationship is experiences shared when we were young, time spent with old friends really helps to remind us who we were back then, and to understand what we became and perhaps even why. And if you and your old friend turned out so differently, as you probably did, it helps you understand and appreciate the other forces and people in your life who steered you in a different direction—for better or for worse.

Someone once said that for everything you gain in life, you lose something, and vice versa. Reconnecting with old friends helps us see how our choices turned out. Seeing an old friend who faced similar choices but chose to go in a different direction can make us a wee bit jealous, or a wee bit appreciative, or—in the best of all worlds—a wee bit of both.

So here's to those old friends who have, in one way or another, helped us live through our good times and our crises; who were always there when we thought we had no one; and who—as painful as this is—may have aged a helluva lot better than we have. Here's to those life-long, womb-to-tomb friends.

You know who you are.

9

FAMILY TIES, FAMILY KNOTS

As baby boomers in the early 21st Century, most of us have been members of families (the ones we came from, not the ones we created) for a half century or more. Surely we must be experts on the subject of family by now. And even if we're not, we've had enough experience with families to pontificate just a little.

Before there were boomers, so I'm told, families were extended and multigenerational. Kids had not only their parents and siblings nearby, but also grandparents, aunts, uncles and cousins.

Change seems to have arrived around the time we boomers did. People moved to distant cities for schooling and jobs, or just beyond the city limits for space and fresh air. Many of our own parents broke the shackles that had kept them bound under the same roof as their parents. Our generation continued that trend, so that, today, those boomers fortunate enough to still have parents living are not likely to have them living *with us.* But, before too long, the remaining parents of boomers will—sadly—pass from the scene.

That leaves us boomers with our siblings. They may be fellow boomers or a bit older or younger. But however old they are, they are our brothers and sisters, and we love them.

Or, perhaps, we don't. Whether we do or we don't, we are now at an age that we can look back with enough perspective to try and see what went wrong—or didn't—and maybe at least minimize the damage.

It seems that most boomer siblings fall into one of three categories. The first are those who have always (we're talking four or five decades here) shared the kind of honest and open love and caring that we all wish we could have. These "type 1" siblings surely need no advice from the rest of us.

The second group of boomer siblings are those who feign closeness for the sake of their parents. In their heart of hearts, these "type 2" siblings can't stand each other. In many of those cases, the seeds of their animosity were sown by their parents, often because their parents seemed to favor one child over the other, or actually did. Left completely to their own devices, these siblings would probably avoid one another; and after their parents are gone, they probably will.

Finally, there is a third group of siblings who manage to love one another in spite of their parents. These "type 3" siblings seem to have forged a bond that even their parents couldn't break through favoritism or other parenting errors. Sadly, these boomer siblings cannot fully appreciate each other until their parents are gone.

Our siblings are the people who—more than anyone else—are with us for most of our lives. In most cases, they are with us on this earth longer than our parents, our spouses, our children, or our friends. If ever there was a relationship worth nurturing, it is brotherhood and sisterhood.

But there is so much baggage that can and does come between siblings, and so much of it is caused by parents. For those "type 3" boomers (the ones who could love each other but for their parents), the passage of our mothers and fathers may solve the problem, but consider the years that may be wasted before that happens. For those "type 2" boomers who hang together solely for the sake of their parents, now is not a bad time to ponder the future that awaits us and—if a future without siblings looks too depressing—begin to peel away some of the baggage.

For us boomers, it may or may not be too late to salvage the relationships with our own siblings. But one thing we ought to do without delay is realize that *we* may well have poisoned the relationships between our own children, just as many of our parents did with us. And while our own parents—dead or living—may have finished doing their damage, we still have lots of time to cultivate jealousy and animosity between our own kids.

In this most important arena, only time will tell if we baby boomers are really as smart as we think we are.

10

REGRESSION TOWARD THE GENE

A few years before my father died, I went to visit him after not having seen him for some time. I scurried around the airport, where he had said he'd pick me up, and didn't see him until I turned a corner. I then came face to face with someone who looked a lot like my father, but seemed so much older than even my dad's 80-odd years. I was startled by the thought that I had seen my father's ghost before my father had departed from this earth.

I saw that ghost again, some time *after* my father died. It was in my own bathroom, after a particularly sleepless night, when I was in no mood to see anyone. The person I saw this time also looked a lot like I remembered my father, but seemed even older and more washed out than my old man had ever looked. And it scared the heck out of me. It was, of course, the image of myself in the mirror.

One of the overarching themes of the baby boom generation was that wherever it was we were heading, we would never turn into our parents. After all, how could a generation that knew—just *knew*—that it was smarter than all previous generations; that practically *invented* coolness, aerobics, low-fat foods, Rogaine®, and maybe even sex; that pledged back in the '60s not to trust anyone over 30, and swore that it would never become as untrustworthy as our elders—how could the members of *that* generation ever turn into their parents?

We are now at about the age that our parents were when we had finally figured out how badly our parents had screwed up the world. And what do you know? Your old friend, whose mother was a stern martinet, has gradually become a control freak in her own right. The boomer whose dad combed his hair up and over his shiny pate, fooling no one, has been wearing a bad toupee since he was 30, fooling fewer people yet. Your cousin, who had been pretty and petite while her mom sat around eating bonbons, has lost her lifelong battle with her metabolism and is now even bigger than your old aunt ever was.

But it really hits home for me when I get into one of my moods, when I'm sarcastic, intolerant and cheap, all at the same time, and my wife (or, in an interesting recent development, one of my kids) decides to shut it down decisively with the line to which I never have a retort: "You're getting just like your father."

What's this about? Are we boomers destined to be subject to all the charges for which we indicted our parents back in the '60s and '70s? Is it regression toward the gene?

The reality, of course, is that our parents weren't just a collection of flaws. They were a mixed bag, pretty much like all generations. Your old friend's mother was a tough old bird, but she was pretty savvy about current events, politics, and a lot more. The bald guy's bald dad was a ball player extraordinaire. Your old aunt who kept outgrowing her clothes gave all those clothes—and a good deal more—to anyone who ever asked for help. My own old man was a hard-working provider and a devoted husband; he could spot a phony a mile away; and he consistently beat me in Scrabble® for about four decades.

It's a little bit like the news we hear on TV and radio: only the bad stuff is newsworthy, and only disasters make headlines. The parents we are slowly turning into had lots of great qualities, but they didn't get nearly as much attention as the flaws, at least from us. And if we happen to have inherited any of those strengths from our parents, no one is likely to find that remarkable today either.

And if our generation has learned anything from our inability to turn out all that differently from our parents, it should be this: the fruits of *our* generation are apples which, like all apples that came before them, are not likely to fall very far from the tree.

11

OTHERS: SIGNIFICANT AND OTHERWISE

As the new millennium moves along, more and more members of the baby boom generation will be contemplating the prospect—and, for many, the reality—of grandparenthood. But for most boomers, long before they get to play with and spoil those sweet and cuddly little creatures, they will have to make the acquaintance of and cultivate a relationship with an altogether different type of creature.

Yes: the son- or daughter-in-law. And even before these strangers become official members of our families, they will play the nebulous role of "significant other" to our child.

Heaven help us.

Sure, we always assumed, from the time they were toddlers, that our kids would form lasting relationships with someone, some day. As modern, with-it boomers, we accepted the fact (or maybe we didn't) that these relationships might—or might not—be formed with members of the opposite sex. The great open-minded free-thinkers of our generation (or maybe just a couple of kids we knew in college, but haven't seen for years) readily accepted that our kids might "hook up" (something—I've heard—that younger generations do) with someone of a different faith or even a different race.

But those are just abstract concepts. Nothing truly prepares us for that moment when a real, living, breathing, 20-something person actually begins to "keep company" (something—I've heard—that prior generations used to do) with our own offspring.

Now, there is no real reason for this experience to be disconcerting. Sure, some of our kids may dally with wrongos, but hopefully (with just a touch of parental meddling) they move on. No, I'm talking about the significant other that comes home with junior who is bright, attractive, ambitious and kind—the type you'd want to have contributing to your gene pool. What is it about the appearance of these stellar citizens at the side of our own kids that causes so much angst?

Well, this is just a theory, but here it goes. These "significant others" are not just important people in our kids' lives. They are—or at least they should be—the *most important* people in their lives. And this means that we boomers, who for half a century believed to our core that we were the most absolutely, totally important people who had ever trod the earth, are no longer the most important people to even our own kids! *Sacre bleu!*

Of course, no boomer phenomenon would be complete without a healthy dollop of disingenuousness. Aren't we the generation that pronounced our own parents irrelevant back in the '60s? Didn't we shout down their music? Their sexual mores? Their politics? Their conformity? Weren't we—the generation that is now inching toward 60—the ones who pronounced that anyone over 30 couldn't be trusted?

So it should surprise no one—least of all us boomers—that these kids of ours whose nurturing we took so seriously for so long now find that it is just a wee bit more fun to be with someone who can't remember when Gerald Ford was president—someone who, like them, was raised by and desperately needs to escape from the clutches of baby boomer parents. If we were able to dismiss our parents' entire generation, surely we can deal with just our own kids relegating us to second or third place.

So what will we do? This brings to mind one of the final episodes of the TV show "The Practice," in which a flirtatious woman asks the character played by James Spader whether he's involved with anyone. His answer: "yes, myself—and I think it's getting serious." If we boomers feel a continuing need to be considered significant, we should probably look for the same sort of admirers we've sought out all our lives:

Other boomers, of course. Luckily, there are still plenty of us left. And if our kids insist on considering someone else more "significant" than us, this might well be an opportune moment for us to follow one of the basic tenets of their generation:

Get over it.

12

FIVE DEGREES OF SEPARATION (AND DROPPING)

Most boomers are probably familiar with the concept of "Six Degrees of Separation." It originated with an experiment conducted in 1967 by a psychologist named Stanley Milgram. The idea was that any two people can be linked up through a chain of connections or relationships where A knows B, B knows C, C knows D, and so forth.

On behalf of the baby boom generation, I demand a recount.

Dr. Milgram's theory may well remain valid insofar as we are talking about the number of degrees of separation between, say, a high school student in Buenos Aires and an octogenarian on the steppes of Central Asia. But if we are talking about the degrees of separation between members of the baby boom generation in the United States, I contend that the number of degrees of separation may be down to five, four or even fewer. In fact, it sometimes seems as though any two boomers who have never met before can find one mutual friend or acquaintance that links the two of them together.

How did this happen? I think it came about because boomers have had many life experiences which have exposed them to large numbers of people. And the more people two boomers know during their lives, the more likely it is that they will have an acquaintance in common.

For example, take college. Members of the baby boom generation had the opportunity to attend college in record numbers. So if a boomer meets someone new and learns that this person went to the University of Wisconsin, chances are the first boomer had a high school classmate who went there around the same time. *Connection!* And a good number of us had the opportunity to go on to graduate school or professional school, creating still more networks of colleagues, acquaintances, and (in some cases) people we remember simply because they were so offensive.

Still further, boomers have had opportunities to travel which far exceeded those of our parents. And, on top of that, boomers have moved around to a considerable degree. Back in the '60s, it seemed as though everyone had spent some time living in Boston, or San Francisco, or even both.

Or take work experience. Boomers have moved from one job to the next with far more ease than prior generations (although younger generations are likely to make us look stable by comparison). As our generation got older and moved around to different employers, still further opportunities were created to decrease the number of degrees of separation between us and the rest of our generation. ("You say you worked at Texas Instruments in Dallas in the late 1980s? Did you know....?")

Or consider what are affectionately known as "extracurricular activities." When we boomers were kids, many of us were involved in activities such as scouting and the like. But consider how our network of acquaintances mushroomed as a result of the extracurricular activities *of our kids*. Every time one of us took Junior to a soccer game or a dance recital, we met up with other boomers who were doing the same.

And let's not forget about the well-documented propensity of baby boomers to move from one marriage to another. Whereas earlier generations had to go through life having only one set of in-laws, boomers may accumulate two, three or more sets. ("Linda Jones is your ex-husband's cousin? What a coincidence! My second wife's nephew is married to Linda Jones' daughter!")

Of course, all of the foregoing does not take into account the impact of modern forms of communication. For example, if you take any two boomers, there is a strong possibility that at some time or other they received an e-mail from the same intermediary; and if we include spammers, the odds become overwhelming. And it seems as though chat rooms have given boomers an opportunity to finally make the acquaintance of the half-dozen or so other boomers they have never run across previously.

Without question, the numerous connections boomers make in the course of their lives will decrease the degrees of separation between boomers and others. Whether this phenomenon has had any benefit remains to be seen.

13

SHAKE HANDS WITH YOUR UNCLE MAX ...

Recall, if you can still think back that far, when you were a youngster back around the late 1950s—say, when you were 11 or 12 years old. Once in a blue moon, your parents would dress you up and drag you off to a wedding or some other big deal "affair." You would leave the TV show you were watching, put on some faux-grownup get-up, and head off to the catering hall.

And there you would be introduced, or reintroduced, to a dazzling array of unctuous uncles, ant-like aunts, and an assortment of other Runyonesque "adults" connected to your family by dubious bloodlines, long-defunct marriages, and sketchy business affiliations.

What a bunch! There was fat old Uncle Fluff, who kept up his weight by positioning himself during the cocktail hour just outside the door to the kitchen, so he could be the first to ambush the waiter and relieve him of a half-dozen hot and fresh pigs in blankets.

Then there was dear Aunt Bombshell. The old harpy had been over the hill for 20 or 30 years, but hadn't gotten the message. Overdressed and bejeweled beyond all reason, she would hit on every attached or unattached male under the age of 93.

And of course there was your dad's business partner, Bill Blowhard, who miraculously knew everything, from where to get the best tuna salad we're talking *his* place, which has *the best*, anywhere on the *planet*—to why you should buy all the Penn Central stock you can get your hands on.

Of course, let's not forget Second Cousin Babka from Baltimore. You and your cousins would spend the entire affair hiding from her, because if she caught you, the old bag, surrounded by a fog of cheap perfume and exuding unfiltered cigarette breath, would plant a big, fat, sloppy kiss on your lips.

All of this is by way of asking you boomers: have you been to a wedding or similar affair *lately*? If you did, did you happen to notice any youngsters—kids who are, say, 11 or 12 years old? Did they appear to have been dragged away from their Gameboys under duress? Were they wearing clothes they obviously had never worn before?

And did it occur to you what those poor kids must be thinking about you and the passel of other boomers milling around at the cocktail hour? Might you have wondered who had been chosen by central casting to play the oppressively offensive "adults" at this 21st century event?

Let's start with boomer Aunt Anorexia, who (on the advice of her personal trainer and her dietician) eats only cholesterol-free, organic Bibb lettuce, washed down with steam made from bottled water. The caterer must make a fortune on the old broad.

But the score gets evened by her husband, boomer Uncle Blob. The sushi he wolfs down in one cocktail hour consumes enough eels to light up a small town. And let's not even discuss the dessert-and-cappuccino table.

And—as luck would have it—Bob Blowhard's boomer son Butthead (who considered a career as a brain surgeon, but instead lived long enough to inherit the old man's business) is in attendance. And he's there to tell you and anyone else who listens who makes the best duct tape anywhere—we're talking *the best*—and why you should accumulate as much Enron stock as you can.

And wait! There's Babka's beloved boomer daughter, Blanche. She was a big-time hippie back in the '60s. Today, she looks like she never came down from her last acid trip. And her dashiki looks like it hasn't seen the inside of the dry cleaner since she moved back east from Haight-Ashbury.

So if we think we're more interesting—or even slightly less nauseating—to kids today than the old bunch was to us a generation ago, we've got another big, whopping think coming.

And so if you see some poor 11- or 12-year-old suffering through an excruciating, interminable affair, who wants to be there a whole lot less than you do, give the poor kid a break—and a large helping of space.

14

MEET THE PARENTS

Some time ago, we examined the phenomenon experienced by many baby boomers whose children had come to acquire "significant others," who—to our consternation—actually turned out to be more "significant" to our kids than we are. But no sooner do we boomers adjust to that change of status than a new challenge looms on the horizon.

In particular, sometimes those relationships formed by our kids get taken to what is today affectionately called "the next level," or what we sometimes refer to as cohabitation, engagement and marriage. And what happens then? Suddenly, Junior no longer has just one set of parents. Now there are *two* people called "Mom" and *two* people called "Dad."

So all of a sudden, at a time in our lives when our circle of friends has remained largely stable for decades, we are thrust into relationships with people we hardly know. We may someday share grandchildren with these people who we've barely just met.

And who knows how much we will have in common with these strangers? This being the 21st century, these folks may be of a different faith, or perhaps even of a different race. They could be older than us (perhaps even too old to be boomers), but then again, they could be younger. They could be better looking. They could be more successful. They could be richer. They could be cooler. They may even turn out to be *all of the above.*

Getting to know these folks would be awkward under any circumstances. But the beginning of this relationship comes at a tumultuous time. Weddings must be planned to satisfy the needs of two families. The kids have to decide where they will be living, and—like it or not—they are going to live closer to one set of parents than the other. The kids may also face career choices, decisions about when (or even whether) to have children, and all that stuff that we thought we had outgrown long ago. And while all this is playing out, while we tiptoe around on our best behavior, trying to make a good impression on these new people in

our lives, life goes on for us boomers. We still have to deal with elevated cholesterol, late charges on our credit card bills, and the plumber not showing up—and
that's just the easy stuff.

It seems like only yesterday—because it was—that our kids were competing
for our attention. Are we now heading into a phase in which *we* will be competing for attention with the "other" parents? And let's take it one step further to the
logical conclusion: when the grandchildren make their appearance, are we going
to be competing with the "other" grandparents to see who become the preferred
babysitters?

I have answers to none of these questions. Searching for something to com-
pare this with, I first tried to think of it as a blind date, where one is forced to
behave one's self even if there turns out to be no attraction. But even the worst
blind dates typically last no longer than an evening.

I now tend to think of it as being somewhat akin to the arranged marriages
that exist in many cultures. But instead of the parents deciding who the kids
should be matched up with, the tables are turned: it is the kids who really
"arrange" the relationship between the two sets of parents. The good news is that
most of those arranged marriages worked out pretty well—because they had to.

We've all heard horror stories about how the two sets of boomer parents of a
young couple got acquainted, spent time together, and eventually grew to despise
each other. The next time they will see each other is at their grandchildren's weddings—if then.

On the other hand, sometimes the two sets of parents get along so well they
think of each other as "family." But this, too, carries some risks. I've heard of situations where the two sets of parents became close friends who often spent time
together. They really and truly got along famously.

Unfortunately, the newlyweds didn't.

Oops!

15

MORE WORLDS, MORE COLLISIONS

In one of my many favorite episodes of *Seinfeld*, hapless George Costanza has, at long last, established a relationship with a member of the opposite sex. But he goes to great pains to keep that segment of his life separate from his antics with Jerry, Kramer and Elaine. After all, if the two should come into contact with each other, "*worlds collide!*"

Star-crossed as he was, George actually had a point. We all live in a number of separate "worlds" that often do not mix very well. And for aging baby boomers, the number of worlds we inhabit seems to be growing exponentially, to the point that compartmentalizing our lives and avoiding collisions can become a full-time job.

It starts early. As a young kid hanging out with other guys, I learned quickly that it was not particularly judicious to tell my parents that my pals and I had frittered away hours at a local newsstand sneaking peaks at *Playboy* centerfolds. Of course, we could never actually *buy* a copy, for where would we keep it, other than in the alien worlds of family homes?

More worlds were created when dating began. On those occasions when I finally worked up the nerve to call up a girl for a date, I wasn't about to do so in the world of my parents' small apartment, with a single phone line and an "extension" which invited eavesdropping. So in order to keep those worlds separate, armed with a pocket full of change, I would trek to a local luncheonette with an indoor phone booth having a door that actually stayed closed, and prepay to an obscene degree, just so that the operator wouldn't interrupt the call, demand another nickel, and blow my cover. Needless to say, I never left a call-back number.

The number of worlds in my life continued to multiply after high school. College was one big new world, but it included smaller sub-worlds, including my freshmen dorm, my fraternity, and the people in my major.

And then we moved on to the world of work. Every workplace is a world unto itself, with its own culture and its unique characters. And if you mix your work world with another one of your worlds, you do so at your own peril.

But all these collisions are nothing compared to what can only be described as the "big bang": marriage. You and your spouse may be kindred spirits, but can anything good possibly happen when you bring together two entire extended families, each of which is at least a wee bit dysfunctional, if only in the eyes of the other? You may have to invite both families to your wedding, but there is one very good reason why weddings always feature an aisle with two well-defined sides, and it has nothing to do with providing a route for the wedding party to parade. Think Mason-Dixon Line, or perhaps the Berlin Wall.

But we boomers who thought we had all of our worlds safely balanced and distanced from each other as we approached the big six-oh have had a rude awakening. When one of our kids finds a mate, that mate brings along a whole 'nother world. And if we have two or—omigosh—even more kids, *each* bringing another world into our orbit, we've got ourselves a veritable galaxy of planets, moons, suns, comets, meteors, and the like on our hands. The laws of probability may say a collision is unlikely, but Murphy's Law says otherwise.

Sooner or later, though, for every one of us boomers, all of our worlds will come together for one brief time. For boomers, as the laws of actuarial science play themselves out, it is beginning to happen more and more frequently. If you've led a full and rich life, the time is going to come, sooner or later, when all of your worlds are going to converge into one small space for perhaps an hour.

Too bad we don't get to watch the fireworks.

Lifestyles Of The Aging And Quirky

16

HAVE STUFF, MAY TRAVEL

Remember when we boomers began to travel in earnest, some four decades ago? We could throw a few things in a satchel, grab our tickets, pop into the airport a few minutes before take-off, and fly away.

We traveled light in those days. I recall one old buddy making an overnight pit stop at my house and showing up with nothing but a toothbrush sticking out of his back pocket. I also remember moving out of school and being able to fit all my earthly possessions into a mid-size car—and still having room to give a friend a lift.

Of course, travel has become more complicated for everyone these days, and not just for boomers. Forget showing up at the airport just before flight time; instead, you'll need to take an extra half day of vacation just to be safe. And if those few things in your satchel include a nail clipper, either you or the nail clipper better plan on staying home. The closest thing to real progress is e-tickets: you needn't remember to pack them; but some of us (myself included) still feel queasy unless we have a ticket that comes with carbon copies (remember *them*?).

Of course, forget about traveling light. As we boomers have gotten older, we seem to need more and more *stuff* when we leave home. I, who couldn't stay awake for a full day of college classes back in the '60s, now need my blindfolds to sleep—especially in a strange bed. And what about our meds? What boomer would leave home without his or her cholesterol medicine? And in case we do have a coronary event on the road, let's not forget our medical insurance card, without which we may be turned away at some distant hospital. And to help minimize the risk of such an event, let's not forget stuff for exercise: sneakers (sorry: "running shoes"), sweats, and perhaps a Walkman® (plus extra batteries, just in case).

And who travels today without a cell phone? That's not the only piece of electronic wizardry we boomers take on trips. Someone who is near and dear to me won't get on a plane without her phone, her PDA and her laptop computer (including, of course, separate chargers for each one), plus a bottle of designer water, at least one can of caffeine-free diet soda, and a snack or two. Her carry-on bag could be used as an anchor for a Nimitz-class aircraft carrier. I affectionately call her the seatmate from hell. What the airport security people and the cabin crews call her cannot be repeated here.

For Richard Boone's old TV character, Paladin, it was "Have Gun, Will Travel." Today, for boomers, it is "Have Tons of Stuff (But Surely No Gun), Will Travel If Not Bumped From Overbooked Flight."

When we were younger, many of us thought that when we approached our golden years, we would have less responsibility, more time, and more money to travel. But it isn't exactly working out that way for many boomers. The economic times, the heightened dangers of travel, and pesky responsibilities like mortgage payments make it tougher than we imagined to get away and pay for it. And while it is possible to find travel bargains, it usually entails things like a minimum stay of 3 nights with a maximum stay of 2 nights; routing from the Northeast to Florida by way of Butte, Montana; and—by the way—you had to buy those tickets (non-refundable, of course) during the previous millennium.

But my favorite boomer travelers are the serious road warriors. You know who I mean: the folks who are in the air nearly every week. The veteran travelers who, in a blind taste test, can distinguish Continental peanuts from those offered by United. One boomer I know has so many miles accumulated that he's planning a hostile takeover of a major domestic airline. For these new-wave travelers, the goal is not retirement, but enough miles in their frequent flier accounts to spend the rest of their days on crowded planes and in bleak airport lounges.

It all sounds to me like a prison sentence with time *added* for good behavior.

17

STRANGER IN A YOUNG LAND

The first time it happened to me, I was in my mid-40s, settling in to what I thought was the heart of middle age.

It happened at a Manhattan restaurant. It was a typical New York eatery: good food; a bit pricey; and trendy, but not painfully so. There was just one big dining room, and we were seated near one side, so that as I sat with my back near the wall, I could see pretty much all of the patrons and all of the staff.

As my wife and our friends studied the menu, I scanned the crowd. And as I looked from one cluster of yuppies to another and, finally, back to my dinner companions, I came to this horrifying realization: *I was the oldest person in the joint!* Older than everyone at my table, older than all the other patrons, *much* older than the waiters and waitresses, and even older than the guy running the place.

No, I'm no expert on people's ages; and yes, there were a couple of people there of "indeterminate age": they might have been in their mid-40s like I was then, but it was equally possible that they were in their late 20s, and my best guess pegged them as 30-something.

I can still recall some four decades earlier when, as a little boy, I was taken to restaurants and was the *youngest* person present. But how did I go from one extreme to the other in just 40 years? The oldest person in any restaurant or any other public place ought to be pushing 70 or 80. How had I achieved codgerdom at such a young age?

I came to understand that my fatal error that evening was trespassing into territory claimed by Generation X and other assorted youngsters. I now realize that in certain precincts of Manhattan and other similar urban centers, a visiting boomer instantaneously becomes the oldest person in the entire zip code.

Of course, there is another side to this coin. Do you want to be the *youngest* kid on the block again? Grab the next plane to Florida. There are some neighborhoods in the Sunshine State where a boomer with dark hair, dark glasses and a well-camouflaged physique who goes to buy a six-pack of beer might be carded by the octogenarian proprietor.

There are strategies that can help us avoid being the oldest person on the premises. For example, avoid all hip coffee bars. Most of the people who patronize them (and *all* of the employees) are too young to remember that a cup of coffee should cost less than a buck. When you ask for decaf and they all look at you, you'll feel like you're 85.

Also, stay away from internet cafes. Even if you know how to navigate your way into your e-mail at work, you will look like you're too old to figure it out. Be especially careful not to talk to the kids who work at these places: when they hear the foreign language you speak, they'll *know*.

And whatever you do, avoid venues where athletic prowess is on display, like batting cages. Sure, you were a pretty good hitter back in the Eisenhower administration. So was Mickey Mantle. Neither of you is going to hit a home run now, and when you fan on every pitch, you'll stick out like a sore thumb. Act your age and repair to the driving range; at least there you'll just be a klutz, but not an *old* klutz.

I'm sure that not every boomer has had the epiphanic experience I first had some fifteen years ago (and have had many times since) of being the oldest person in a group. I'm equally certain that there are many boomers who may well have been the oldest person present somewhere, but didn't even realize it, or just didn't care because they've adjusted to aging better than I have.

As for me, I'll keep eating in restaurants frequented by younger people, and hope for the best. If I'm lucky, my advancing age might get me a better table. And if I'm *really* lucky, the maitre d' won't tell me I'm too late for the early bird special.

18

SNOBBERY, BOOMER STYLE

In "Snobbery: The American Version," Joseph Epstein takes a comprehensive look at how snobbery has evolved in the United States. He describes how snobbery based on lineage has been replaced with new snobberies based on education, connections, and even self-selected morally superior views (held by what Epstein calls "virtucrats").

But Mr. Epstein, who was born before "the war" rather than after it, may not have fully appreciated the unique nuances of snobbery as practiced today by the generation that was weaned on the 60's dogma that we are all—supposedly—equal in all ways. So today we take a peek at snobbery, boomer style.

We begin, of course, with money. "Old" money doesn't cut it with boomers; that's a throwback to "lineage." And "new" money alone doesn't buy elitism today. After all, back in the 90's dot-com frenzy, kids half our age made "new" money hand over fist.

With boomers, it's *quiet* money that counts: money that doesn't shout, but whispers just loud enough for us to know it's there. You know the type: the boomer who drives a well-worn Saab when you know he could afford a Benz. Or take housing. No self-respecting boomer snob would be caught dead living in a McMansion. After all, any wretch with a down payment and low mortgage rates could leverage himself into one of those suckers. The serious boomer snob's house isn't flashy, but it's always in a *very* "desirable" location. If home is an apartment, don't even think about a rental or a condo; after all, you don't get approved by a board to live in those places. Only a co-op will do, and only in certain "quality" buildings.

The boomer snob will brag about her kids as much as the next person. Telling everyone about your boy at Duke or Dartmouth still works, but let's face it: lots of successful boomers have kids who really can't cut it. This has led to the phenomenon of kid-based snobbery based on spin.

Take the boomer who brags about his daughter who was in a "special pro-gram" consisting of a year studying comparative native crafts, followed by an "externship" in the hospitality industry, and then finishing up studying criminal justice. (*Translation: she flunked out of basket weaving, had to take a semester off flipping burgers, and is now doing time in a minimum security prison for possession of drugs.*)

Or take the boomer snob who combines spin and namedropping like, say, the one whose son "works for Arnold Schwarzenegger." (*Translation: he's a clerk at motor vehicles in Bakersfield.*)

Watch out for boomer braggarts who try to impress you with the cachet of the exotic places their kids live in, like the matron whose daughter is selling taco-fla-vored Twizzlers in Tierra Del Fuego. (*Translation: the poor girl was so suffocated by her mother that she headed south and never stopped.*)

Keep a sharp eye out for the blowhard boomers whose boasts about Junior are literally true, but there's less than meets the eye, like the lady at your club whose kid is "producing movies." (*Translation: he works at the factory, covering DVDs with that plastic packaging that only a surgeon can remove.*)

The boomer snob doesn't fritter away time on something purely recreational, such as golf or—heaven forbid—watching TV. Her time is too *valuable*. She doesn't work long hours, since that might give the incorrect impression that she needs the money. So she's busy with other, more *significant* stuff, like writing a symphony, raising money for relief efforts in some currently fashionable third-world country, *and*—simultaneously and single-handedly—curing juvenile dia-betes. The only break she takes is to tell people—actually, quite a few peo-ple—about all of this.

Boomers didn't invent snobbery. But boomers have been particularly creative about breaking new ground in snobbery as our generation has aged. This is why everyone should watch out for lines like this, which we'll soon be hearing: *Did I mention that my grandson started walking at the age of two weeks, and is now leading a march on Washington seeking to lower the voting age to six?....*

19

SHOW ME THE MONEY

The baby boom generation has had an on-again, off-again relationship with money. In the 60s and 70s, rebellious boomers shunned money as the root of all evil. By the 80s and 90s, we had gotten religion, working hard to accumulate it, spend it, or both. Today, boomers are worrying about whether they'll have enough of it to educate their kids, help their parents, and have something left for themselves.

But there is one aspect of money that took off in one direction when we were young and has continued unerringly in that same direction: the diminishing role of *cash*.

You remember cash, don't you? Big bills, small bills and even coins? Our first allowances were in cash. The first money we earned at part-time jobs came as bills and coins. My first penny-and-two poker games were played with real pennies.

Then, around our adolescence, came the earliest credit cards. At first, few merchants accepted them, and consumers tried them warily. I recall my mother getting her first "Bankamericard" from our local bank. With great trepidation, she charged her first purchase, and then walked straight to the bank to pay her debt.

We all know the next part of the story. Credit cards took over everything. One by one, the barriers fell in places like supermarkets. Eventually, our plastic cards were often not even processed by people but by machines, which sold us stuff like train tickets and gasoline.

And just in case we weren't using our credit cards enough, along came incentives like airline mileage linked to our credit card usage. Who'd be crazy enough to pay cash and pass up "free" mileage? And in case we were getting maxed out on our existing cards, there were offers of new cards in the mail. *Lots* of offers, *every* day.

Where has this led us? For a lot of boomers, it has led us into a mountain of debt. We all know horror stories of people who keep accumulating cards, maxing them out, making only the minimum payment, and building debts that may never get paid off. Boomers didn't invent debt, but they sure did elevate debt to dizzying heights.

The real question is whether the baby boom generation will actually see the beginning of a truly cashless society. Coins may be the first to go. I used to carry a pocketful of change for pay phones (an endangered species since cell phones came along) and tolls (now paid through EZ-PASS). I used to think parking meters would be the last stronghold of coin usage, but I've seen articles suggesting that it's just a matter of time.

When and where will we see the last of paper money? Taxicabs seem like good candidates for the last holdout. Will we start to get those credit card slips that restaurants use, with a space for a tip? Will we screw up the arithmetic while the person who wants your cab next tries to scurry you out? Prediction: taxi meters will develop slots to receive our cards when we enter, and will spit out our card when we arrive, along with a receipt (and a 15% tip automatically added).

And what about those tips that are not tied in with a larger purchase, like the ones we give the kid who valet parks our car? Or the guy who checks in our bags at the airport?

Today, I can do a round of errands like filling the tank, picking up the dry cleaning, shopping at the market, and more, with no cash. But what about the sweet kids who camp outside the market to raise funds for soccer teams, bands, you name it. They don't take credit cards—yet.

A time will come—and I think it will arrive while we boomers are still around—when cash becomes a memory, and we will get one depressing 20-page statement listing every nickel we spent for an entire month. There will still be expenditures listed which we don't remember and merchants we've never heard of, just *more* of them. And we will write a check (assuming *checks* still exist) for the minimum balance.

Will it really happen in our time? Who knows? Flip a coin—while you still have one.

20

CALL ME

The baby boom generation has seen amazing advances in technology since our youth. Nothing illustrates this better than telephones. And as the technology has evolved, so has our relationship with it.

I remember well the first phone my family had. I here use the singular form, rather than the plural, quite deliberately. We had one black phone with a rotary dial that was hardwired to the wall. On those rare occasions that we experienced a problem, we simply called "the phone company" (again, the use of the singular is deliberate), whereupon our clunky old phone was cheerfully repaired or replaced.

Where I grew up, you were only entitled to a limited number of local calls every months. I think they used to call them "message units." Thus, when you made a call, you disposed of the pleasantries and your business quickly, and hung up the phone to turn the meter off. A "long-distance call" was perceived as a major expenditure. On those rare occasions when a family member was out of town, you spoke just long enough to confirm that they had arrived safely, and that was about it.

The changes in telephone technology were initially modest. I recall my family's excitement when we first got an "extension" phone, which enabled two people to talk to that out-of-town traveler simultaneously, thus saving time and—not incidentally—long-distance charges.

That clunky black phone changed slowly as well. Colors other than basic black were one major breakthrough, but that was nothing compared to the smaller and more streamlined "Princess" phone, which still had only a rotary dial.

Fast forward now to the 1990s. The first mobile phones I had were designed to be used in a car, and I called them (and sometimes still call them) car phones. Only gradually did it dawn on me that I could have a mobile phone without having to purchase a car as an accessory.

Fast forward once again to the early 21st century. It seems like virtually everyone, everywhere, young and old, has a cell phone. This never ceases to amaze me, since I can still recall those days when only fictional detective Dick Tracy, with his two-way wrist radio, could have "wireless" conversations. And the technology in cell phones today is bewildering (at least to this boomer) in complexity. With all the stuff I can do with my phone (play games, take pictures, send text messages, etc.), I feel like such a dinosaur when I make a plain old phone call.

Perhaps the biggest change is that no one today feels the need to get off the phone quickly. With payment plans juiced up with "free" minutes, boomers seem bound and determined to make up for those abbreviated calls of their youth by staying on the phone forever. It seems like any time of any day, I can be driving along the highway and the driver in the next lane over is on the phone for the entire trip. Even after the ride ends, the call does not. I routinely see people in parking lots with cell phones cradled in their necks, talking or listening, or sometimes just breathing.

But as in all other aspects of life, cell phones involve a tradeoff. We boomers love the security of knowing we can place a call anytime we want from wherever we may be. But the problem now is that we are always expected to carry our cell phones, and there is nowhere to hide from our bosses, clients, spouses, creditors and anyone else who wants our attention. And if you want to give up any last vestige of peace and tranquility, get yourself one of those cell phones (or whatever you call them) that allows you to get e-mails. Imagine! Spam! 24-7! On any continent!

If there has been one constant theme in the baby boom generation, it has been that we always have a great deal to say. Strong silent types—and even weak silent types—need not apply. The cell phone revolution allows us to talk at any time, wherever we may be, for hours on end. Which leaves me with just one question.

Who has the time and the patience to *listen* to all that blather?

21

FREEDOM OF TOO MUCH CHOICE

One of the most ballyhooed phenomena of the last decade or two has been the proliferation of choices in areas where, in earlier eras, there had been little or none. You see it practically everywhere. Some of us boomers are becoming overwhelmed. I know I am. CBS News has called it Option Fatigue, an under-diagnosed social disease.

Take TV for example. As kids, we boomers had a half dozen or so channels to choose from, some of which showed mostly old movies, and one of which was (*gulp!*) educational. If none of those choices interested us, our parents would kick us out of the house to—perish the thought—get some fresh air. But as time marched on, first those curious UHF channels on the far side of channel 13 came into view. Then there was cable, satellite and technologies with, seemingly, more channels than there are viewers.

For that matter, consider the question of TV sets. It used to be that you just had to choose a size and—later—select color or black and white. Today, you need to decide if you want high-definition, flat screen, plasma, or some other technology you (or at least I) don't understand.

Or consider cars. When we were kids, if someone wanted to buy a car in a certain price range, they chose between an Oldsmobile, a Mercury and a Dodge. Today, there must be 20-odd brands, each offering sedans, SUVs, and specialty vehicles ranging from hybrid-powered in-line skates to lunar rovers. You can drive darn near anything (except, alas, an Oldsmobile).

Or take something as simple as soft drinks. Once, there were Coke and Pepsi, period. Today, there must be a dozen varieties of each, not to mention green and not-so-green teas, designer waters (with and without fruit flavors, carbonation, caffeine and nitroglycerine), and assorted "sports" drinks they tell you to consume before colonoscopies. I'm fully expecting to see co-branding combos like a bottle of diet extra-caffeinated pistachio Coke joined at the hip with a bag of whole grain paprika-flavored Doritos.

Of course, the Internet has taken freedom of choice to levels that were unimaginable when we were younger. Think about newspapers for a moment. When we were young, most bigger cities had a few competing papers, and that small number shrank for a while. But today, if you want, you can read virtually *every* paper in *every* city, as well as papers in languages you can't even recognize, through a few clicks of your mouse and without even smudging your hands. Imagine! If you have the time (and you should get help if you do), you can now read virtually every word written about Paris Hilton and Michael Jackson.

I began to realize that I wasn't cut out for a world with too much choice a number of years ago, when I needed a new book to read. I first went to a book store that was maybe half the size of a modern Borders. I traipsed all over, from department to department, became totally paralyzed by indecision, and finally left empty handed. But a day or two later, while in a drug store to pick up a tube of toothpaste (back when you didn't have to choose between tartar control, whiteners, extra mouthwash, etc.), at a rotating rack with maybe 30 paperbacks, I found the perfect read. (Good thing I didn't have to choose among the 679,231 different shampoos that were offered.)

The younger generations seem to thrive on all this choice. They can't imagine a world without it. But for me, and perhaps some fellow boomers, it's just too much to process at my age.

Here's what I mean. A while back, I was taken to a new Asian restaurant. After poring through a menu the size of *Anna Karenina*, I found a dish that sounded good, and it was. But I'll never get to enjoy it again, because I simply can't remember (a) the name of the dish, or (b) the dish's ingredients, or (c) the name of the restaurant, or (d) the location of the restaurant, or even (e) the specific cuisine. Was it Thai? Vietnamese? Korean?

At my age, it's all Asian Confusion.

22

MODERN MATURITY?

They eat sugary desserts and fat-larded snacks with apparent abandon.

They watch the most juvenile movies, over and over again.

They love small, fast, overpriced cars that seem to guzzle 20 gallons per mile.

They have absolutely no concept of the value of money, which they spend like drunken sailors.

They take risks that seem hazardous and often get away with them through nothing but sheer luck.

We're talking about adolescents, right? We're talking about our kids (if we started late) or maybe they're our grandkids (if we started early), aren't we? They're in their late teens, these immature creatures, right? Or maybe, at most, their early 20s?

No, the people I'm talking about are a little older. Actually, they're *a lot* older. Come to think of it, these immature brats are members of the baby boom generation. They're us.

Yes, today we're talking about people in their 50s and even pushing into the uncharted waters of 60-plus. And by some definitions, according to some social arbiters, their behavior would be considered downright immature. It sometimes seems that someone needs to cry out, *is there a grown-up in the house?....*

I remember first hearing about maturity back around fifth grade. Maturity was one of those many qualities I didn't have back then and seemed destined to never acquire. At a time when appearing "grown up" seemed immeasurably important, there was no greater curse than being tagged as immature. Trust me, I know.

The problem was particularly acute for us males. There was a popular song back in the 1960s called "Girls Grow Up Faster Than Boys." The girls who attended school with me (it would be a stretch to refer to them as the girls with whom I socialized) never let us boys (or maybe just *this* boy) forget it.

But the waves of people born after World War II moved into college, and then moved into the work force, and then started families. Now, as the dust starts to settle, and we see that we've moved well past halftime in life, a lot of boomers are starting to do those things they couldn't afford to do, or were afraid to do. They are also doing things they just plain *wouldn't* do as kids, lest they be called immature.

Those sweet desserts and cardio-toxic snacks? The chocoholic boomers I know who indulge in these indiscretions only do it once in a while—albeit with great fanfare—but when you're not looking, they eat boring, whole grain fat-emulsifying organic salads and prepay for the next indulgence on the treadmill.

Those embarrassingly stupid movies? The boomers I know who watch all Steven Seagal films whenever they pop up on cable (and may even record them on their DVRs) handle huge amounts of responsibility at work and at home. The release they get from watching inanity like *Animal House* sure beats real road trips and toga parties.

Those fast, sporty cars? The boomers I know who drive them can well afford them, as well as the gas they guzzle. And some of those cars end up holding their value better than the sober sedans and SUVs the rest of us drive.

How about all that frivolous spending? Heck, the boomers we're talking about have been working most of their lives—some 30 to 40 years!—and some have no intention of giving up their day jobs. Their kids are off the payroll. They can afford to go overboard now and then—and they do.

And how about those risks? Sure, they seem chancy. But a lot of boomers learned a lot of stuff during the half-century they spent before they started approaching codgerdom. They have a pretty good idea which risks make sense and which ones don't. When some of those risks pay off, it isn't just dumb luck.

Maturity turns out to be a good quality to display at job interviews, or perhaps when meeting your lover's skeptical parents.

But, at the end of the day, maturity turns out to be a wee bit overrated.

23

OUT OF CONTROL

The *New York Times* recently reported—in its Style section, of course—on a remarkable trend in funerals. In an article entitled "It's My Funeral and I'll Serve Ice Cream if I Want To," it was revealed that members of the Baby Boom generation are planning funerals for their parents, and even for themselves, which are not, well, particularly funereal. At these "concierge" funerals, the guests are served Popsicles, marshmallows, or whatever; they ride Harleys and hit golf balls; they limit speeches to three minutes; seating arrangements are carefully considered; and viewing the deceased—considered a "downer"—is minimized.

What's going on here? One funeral industry executive says its just another area where boomers want things personalized and specific to their lives. It's a bit like extending the concept of "have it your way" beyond the realm of fast food.

But another funeral expert quoted in the article views it differently. He says "Baby boomers are all about being in control. This generation wants to control everything ..."

So *that's* it. *Now* we have begun to figure out this generation. After some 60 years of being called spoiled, obnoxious, disrespectful, narcissistic, and lots of other things, we're now accused of being a bunch of control freaks.

Can this possibly be true? Well, it *is* true that a few of us have been known to program our children just a wee bit (like choosing their playmates, colleges, careers, and even spouses where we can). And maybe—just maybe—a few boomers in positions of authority have been guilty of "hands-on" management, meddling just a tad in what our underlings do at the workplace (and—in the most rare instances—in their free time).

And yes, we've been known to control things like our environment. It took the tobacco industry about 200 years to get people smoking in every office. And it took us boomers about one generation to clear the air.

So let's accept the fact that perhaps there's a kernel of truth in that funeral maven's assertion that the boomer generation is all about control. If he's right, the really interesting question is *why* this came to pass.

My theory is that boomers came to need control because, when we were coming of age, we had control over nothing.

As kids in the Eisenhower era, we watched our parents conform to societal norms, and were told that we could expect to do the same when we grew up. We could do anything we wanted, so long as it was acceptable to the arbiters of taste, style, manners, and decorum. Grow your hair long? *Please!* Skip college and become a carpenter? *Fuhgedaboudit!*

But all this was just a warm-up for the main event: the Vietnam War, fueled by General Hershey's military draft. A bunch of white (and only white) middle-aged guys (and only guys) in suits in Washington shipped youngsters of all shapes, sizes, and colors off to fight a war in Asia. And we couldn't vote those guys out of office because of one small problem: we couldn't vote *at all*. It was a question of control. We didn't have any. None.

And so we boomers moved into jobs and families. Silently, and perhaps unconsciously, we sought to gain the control over our lives and our world that had been so sorely lacking in our youth. But when we finally reached an age where we thought we might exercise that control, a depressing reality reared its ugly head: with hundreds of millions of others in this country, and billions of others elsewhere, we boomers of America weren't about to control the world, or even America, not now, not ever.

And so we turned inward, exercising—or at least trying to exercise—control over our microcosms: our families, our subordinates, and the air quality in a few thousand square feet of office space.

Which is why, as boomers move through and beyond middle age, you can expect some boomer to plan her funeral on a Boeing 767, with the flight crew singing, "*I'm leaving on a jet plane ...* " or (with apologies to the *Times*) "*It's my party, and I'll fly if I want to....*"

Boomers Looking Backwards

24

YOU MUST REMEMBER THIS—OR NOT

It isn't funny any more.

You know what I'm talking about. Those lapses in memory, when we can't seem to recall a word, a name, a place, or whatever. You know what we call those increasingly embarrassing black-outs, don't you? Of course *I* know what the expression is—it's on the tip of my tongue—come on, help me out here—oh yes! *Senior moments!*

First of all, there's nothing even remotely amusing about associating the baby boom generation with "senior" *anything*. So what if we get mailings from AARP. Whether we think of ourselves as precocious pups, or whether (as our elders have always told us) we are just spoiled brats, the common theme has always been that we're just a bunch—a very large bunch—of *kids*.

But while our generation still deludes itself about its youthfulness, the simple fact is we're getting older, with all the accoutrements of old age. And one fact that we have to accept is that, some days, we can't remember a damned thing.

Social gatherings of boomers are turning into pathetic spectacles. Lively conversations get derailed as one boomer struggles to remember a word or a name, while the others chime in, trying to help the poor wretch out. It can start to sound like a game of 20 Questions or Charades. "Is it bigger than a breadbox?" "Is it animal, vegetable or mineral?" "Was he Goldwater's running mate?" And by the time the elusive word or name is rediscovered, the interrupted conversation is itself a memory, lost forever by the entire forgetful group. If boomers were to gather at Rick's in Casablanca, no one would be singing, "You must remember this...."

But there is one thing about our forgetfulness which, if not exactly funny, is at least somewhat fascinating: how *selectively* we remember and forget. In contrast to all that stuff we keep forgetting, there are some things which are practically hardwired into our brains. I'm talking music here—*our* music. The music we grew up with. The music of the '50s and '60s.

You know the scene. You hear the first three or four notes of an old '60s song on your car radio, and you not only recognize the song; you can sing the whole darn song, and (somewhat painfully, for those in the car with you) you actually do. And as you and the song wind down, you can't remember the name of the store you were driving to, or why.

What it is about that music? Was it just how great it was? Sure, *we* think it was great, but *we* think all things boomer were better than anything that came before or after.

Or maybe it's because the radio stations keep playing those songs—*our* songs. Some stations seem to have started up in the '60s playing '60s music, and they've played the same '60s music now for over four decades. We've heard those old songs so many times that we'd have to be brain dead *not* to remember them.

I suspect the reason so many radio stations play so many boomer songs is simple marketing. Our generation is still so huge that advertisers will pay dearly for the privilege of allowing us to listen to 40-year-old songs we've already heard hundreds of times. I suspect the only reason we never hear Big Band music from the '40s is that earlier generations are too small and simply lack our marketing clout. Would the advertisers keep on paying for that '60s music if they knew this dirty secret: that we remember the songs—heck, by now, we know them all by heart—but we forget the commercials instantaneously.

It is sometimes said that what we're losing now is just our *short-term* memory. We can remember every word from every Beach Boys song, but we have no clue why we just walked into a room. Which probably explains why we all remember those old songs, while I can't recall the incredibly clever punch line I had in mind for this piece only yesterday. Can someone help me out here?

Like I said: it isn't funny any more.

25

IT WAS A VERY GOOD YEAR

When Frank Sinatra turned 21, we are told in his signature song, it was a time of city girls who lived upstairs, with perfumed hair that came undone. As Mr. Sinatra crooned so mellifluously, it was a *very* good year.

For baby boomers who, like me, turned 21 in 1968, it was American society that came undone that year. The war in Vietnam raged on, with the military draft ratcheting skyward to keep up with the body count. Dr. Martin Luther King, Jr. and Sen. Robert Kennedy were assassinated, touching off riots in inner cities. Civilians were massacred at My Lai. The Democratic convention in Chicago exposed the open wounds in American society, leaving the Democratic party and the democratic process in shambles. The year 1968 culminated in the election of Richard Nixon as President, which surely requires no comment.

Years later, our children would study 1968 in their history classes. Their textbooks officially dubbed it The Year That Everything Went Wrong.

Perhaps you are a slightly younger boomer, who turned 21 in 1970: the year of Mr. Nixon's Cambodian "incursion," and the year that baby boomers in the Ohio National Guard killed other baby boomers at Kent State.

Does this suggest that baby boomers have led a tougher life than Mr. Sinatra's generation? Well, Ol' Blue Eyes tells us that when he was 17, it was another *very* good year. But 1932, when Mr. Sinatra turned 17, was the nadir of the Great Depression, when the stock market dropped to 10% of its 1929 value.

It was supposedly another *very* good year for Mr. Sinatra when he turned 35. But that was 1950, when Sen. Joseph McCarthy began his tirades, and when North Korea invaded the South, touching off three more years of war.

Every generation has years that seem, from a historical vantage, to be particularly good, and other years which seem just awful. But, like most of life, it is never all that clear cut.

Take 1963, when we boomers were around high school age. To our generation, 1963 was the year President Kennedy was assassinated. But 1963 was also
the year in which Dr. King delivered his "I Have A Dream" speech.

Just as no year is *very* good—or *very* bad—in every way on a national level,
every year brings good and bad to boomers and everyone else on a personal level.
Even during chaotic 1968, lots of boomers graduated from college, and many got
married.

Of course, the degree to which a year is very good or not depends a great deal
on the age and past experiences of your generation. The assassination of President
Kennedy was, for us boomers, a shocking wake-up call, teaching us that nothing
in life is ever certain. But for our parents, who had seen FDR die in office when
they were young, it was a different kind of loss: the death of the first president of
their generation, a vibrant man with a large, storied family, including two small
children who would never be the same.

Which is why we need to understand that events which occur as we go
through the bottom half of middle age, such as the bizarre election of 2000, or
the terrorist attacks of 2001, mean one thing to us, and something else altogether
to our children. Will the 2000 election convince them that politics is so rigged
that our children blow off politics altogether? We went through something similar with Watergate, but we now have lived long enough to learn that a generation
gives up on politics at its peril.

And our kids will also come to learn that even horrific events like the 2001 ter-
ror attacks must be viewed in proper perspective. Some day, they will realize that
in addition to all the death and destruction, 2001 was a year in which many of
them graduated from college, fell in love, married, or even made a pair of
boomers into grandparents.

And maybe some day, some son or daughter of boomers, born in 1980 with a
great voice and a penchant for oldies—*real* oldies—will croon, "When I was 21,
it was a *very* good year …"

26

REUNITED STATES

Remember the first time you went to a reunion? Maybe it was five years after you graduated. Many schools make an effort to bring back their "quinquennial" classes, so that first reunion you attended featured not only your classmates celebrating their 5th, but also groups celebrating their 10th, 15th, 20th, and so forth.

And do you recall, back at that first reunion, a little group of codgers who returned to celebrate their 35th or maybe even their 40th? They may have been gray, fat and bald; and without question, they were hopelessly out of date. Depending on your own generosity of spirit, those geezers celebrating their 35th and 40th anniversaries were either adorable or pathetic.

So, fellow boomers, if you are planning to attend a reunion in the next couple of years, guess what role Central Casting has chosen for you and your classmates this time around.

Reunions, of course, were around long before there were boomers. And so were the reunion stories: the crash diets, the cosmetic surgery, the rented jewelry and Porsches, and the desperate efforts to prove to one's former peers that you weren't the loser they expected you to be.

So what could the baby boom generation do to complicate this phenomenon? Well, more of us went to college than in earlier generations, and significant numbers of boomers went on to graduate and professional schools. Thus, where our parents may have had only high school reunions to anticipate or fear, many boomers have two or even three reunion cycles, practically guaranteeing one reunion or another every couple of years.

If—like me—you've attended a fair number of reunions over the years, you've probably discovered by now that, in these reunited states, not all reunions are created equal. I think it started to hit me in 1984, when my high school 20th was followed a week or two later by my graduate school 10th—which worked out well, because the graduate school event got me out of the depression caused by seeing my high school classmates. My college reunions are in a different cycle—years that end in 3 and 8—and I think I went to most of them, and enjoyed them, too. But until recently, I hadn't attended a high school reunion since the Reagan administration.

So here is one boomer—I suspect there are others—who can attend reunions of three different schools and looks forward to two of them, but avoids one like the plague. What gives?

I got a clue when a group from my high school class began talking up our 40th reunion, which was then nearly two years off. They organized one of those e-mail deals, where anyone with anything to say could say it to the whole class of 1964 (or at least those who hadn't fallen off the information highway). Within a week, the chatter drifted away from the reunion and toward more general stuff. And by the third week, I couldn't take it. Aside from the political extremists, which my high school seemed to produce in impressive numbers, and the occasional sociopath, I found myself feeling totally disconnected from these people.

Not unlike the way I felt in 1964.

And then I clicked on "Unsubscribe."

I came to realize that there probably wasn't anything wrong with my high school class. And it wasn't that I didn't like this group of 800 people; I only remembered a small fraction of the people. What it was, was this: I didn't like who *I* was in 1964 all that much. And all these 800 people were doing was reminding me of *that*.

So this fortunate boomer gets to pick and choose the phases of his life that he will revisit in his remaining five-year reunion cycles. I started to really enjoy life in college. And in graduate school, I hooked up with the profession I wanted to work in and the person I wanted to be with for my remaining days. Who *wouldn't* want to revisit those good times and the people with whom you shared them?

And to my high school class: check back with me for our 50th.

27

FOR THE RECORD

Who could resist a chance to see one's very own "permanent record" from grades K through 12? Word arrived that my high school was unloading ancient files, and that for the princely sum of $3 (no checks; cash or money order only), I could get a copy of my own file. It turned out to be sort of an archeological dig through the Eisenhower/Kennedy era of my own life, 1952-1964.

The first thing I pulled out of the envelope sent a chill through me. At the very top of one of the New York City Board of Education forms was a "Loyalty Pledge," in which the student was to declare his or her loyalty not only to the United States, but also to the State of New York. I guess the school's supply of these forms outlasted the McCarthy era, because—I was happy to see—mine wasn't signed. Good thing, too, that I didn't declare my loyalty to New York State, seeing as I haven't lived there for over three decades.

Much of my file pertained to the college application process, including two evaluation forms from teachers I had selected. My math teacher, who completed one of my forms, apparently never knew that it was me who was throwing small pieces of chalk around the room when his back was turned. Or maybe—sweet man that he was—he knew but didn't care.

The other form was completed by my English teacher, one of those truly great teachers that—if you're lucky—you have once in a lifetime. In my senior year, he wrote, "A good English student, tho [his spelling!] *not yet* impressively intellectual." [My emphasis.] I recently learned that he just turned 90. I hope he's not still waiting for me to meet his august expectations.

But the highlight of my file was another document prepared to assist my guidance counselor in writing letters of recommendation to colleges: my autobiography, dated January 2, 1964, in which I dutifully recorded my interests, my views and my plans.

It turns out a few thing haven't changed. Even then, I liked to travel, I loved to tackle the Sunday *Times* crossword puzzle, and I enjoyed writing. In those respects, I was pretty much a done deal some four decades years ago.

My autobiography also made clear that by my senior year in high school, I hated social studies; and—to judge by my grades—it didn't think all that much of me either. With hindsight, I think I just hated the way they force-fed it to us back then. I taught myself a good deal about social studies later in life, but it was too late—*much* too late—to change my permanent record.

But then there was the matter of my politics. At the dawn of LBJ's "Great Society," I described myself as an Ayn Rand conservative-objectivist. From that phase of my life I am still in recovery.

And then there was the selection of a college major (wrong choice) and a career (wrong again). I would spend many years trying to undo those choices, with only limited success. I suppose there are 17-year-olds out there who have the maturity, foresight and self-knowledge to predict what they'd want to be doing 10, 20 or 30 years later. I was not one of them.

In some ways, the most remarkable thing about reading my 1964 autobiography was simply the way it read. When my family read it, they said my style and "voice" were the same then as they are now.

There are several ways you can react to that. For example, maybe I was precocious as an adolescent writer, with abilities beyond my years.

Or maybe I've discovered that, four decades later, with years of higher education, loads of reading, decades of work experience, child rearing, a bit of teaching, and a bunch of life experience—with all that, my writing style hasn't matured beyond where it was in high school.

Or maybe the way to look at it is that there is still hope for me. Maybe if my 90-year-old high school English teacher could read my stuff today, he would *still* say that I'm "not yet" impressively intellectual.

28

GREETINGS!

How's this for a bit of serendipity? Just as the 2004 presidential campaign was focusing on who had served in Vietnam and who had pursued other priorities, coming on the heels of proposals to revive the draft to support the war in Iraq, a household move required that I excavate decades of accumulated detritus in my basement. Out popped a sheaf of correspondence to—and mostly from—my draft board between 1968 and 1970. It all came rushing back, and it did so on a very personal level.

- October 16, 1968 (a few months after graduating from college and a few weeks after quitting a job I hated but had taken only because it seemed likely to land me a deferment): my 1A classification arrives.

- October and November, 1968: letters are sent to my draft board, trying to convince them that the graduate degree I was seeking was in the national interest (!).

- November 13, 1968: notice of my appointment with a "Government Appeal Agent" to obtain advice on Selective Service matters. (The advice I received: get real, kid.)

- February 17, 1969: a notice granting my request for a transfer of my physical exam from the city of my draft board to the city in which I was then living (a common ploy to buy a few weeks—after all, the war could end any day, right?).

- March 14, 1969: order to report for the physical at the new location.

- April 3, 1969: I was "found not acceptable for induction under current standards." (I flunked!)

- March 31, 1970: ordered to report for a *second* physical. (The minor problem that had caused me to flunk the first time was correctable by surgery. Had I gotten the surgery? Take a wild guess.)

- April 23, 1970: found "not acceptable" once again; classified 1Y.

(I omitted the very first document in the sequence: my original draft card, issued the day after I turned 18 in 1965, because it wasn't in my basement. Since the back of the draft card reads, "The law requires you to have this certificate in your personal possession at all times....," and since they never rescinded that order, it remains in my wallet to this day.)

Who can forget the torment caused by the Vietnam War and the draft? So many boomers lost their lives, or limbs, or any prospect of a normal life, during those ugly days. Personal and national schisms developed between those who served and those who didn't.

It was easy back then to say you were avoiding the draft because the war was unjust and unjustified. So many boys of our generation (we hardly could be called men at the time) went over the border or underground to avoid service, or declared themselves conscientious objectors.

But for many of us who wouldn't go that far, draft "avoidance" was sort of a warm-up to the tax "avoidance" antics we would practice years later: if the dodge was legal, you could—and (according to conventional wisdom in many boomer circles) even *should*—take advantage of it. So what if someone less resourceful had to fill your slot. In times like that, it was every man (or should I say boy) for himself.

Three-plus decades later, it doesn't look quite the same. Maybe it's age. Maybe it's the fact that our current war makes Vietnam seem far more important than it did during the Nixon days.

And here's the bad part. As the 2004 campaign wore on, I found my own draft history to be uncomfortably similar to that of the candidates I opposed. To be sure, I opposed them for lots of reasons, but I wonder if I could ever vote for myself (with my own draft-dodging baggage) in an election.

And then there's the very worst part of all. Some 35-odd years after the fact, I can't help wondering whether all the talk about the evils of the Vietnam War was just a smoke screen. Did all the stall tactics grow out of genuine political opposition to the war?

Or was it really just self-interest or perhaps peer pressure? Or—worse yet—was it just a simple case of old-fashioned cowardice?

29

WRITE OR WRONG

Like dog biting man, a boomer whose skills have improved over the years is not exactly newsworthy stuff. We all have things we've gotten better at over the years, whether it be cooking, brain surgery, crossword puzzles, channel surfing, or what have you.

But it *is* a big deal when you find a skill that has *deteriorated* over the decades; an area where your ability in your 30s was worse than it was when you were an adolescent, and even now, as you chase the big six-oh, it is worse than ever.

For me, I need look no further than penmanship.

Remember when we were taught how to put pen (or, even earlier, pencil) to paper? We sat in our elementary school classrooms as our teachers showed us what "cursive" writing was supposed to look like. The teachers were so darned good at it. To me, it was like calligraphy on a chalkboard.

For some of us, writing by hand was never easy. But for me, it was somewhere between painful and pathetic. I am—you may have surmised—an unrecon-structed lefty.

I can still recall those patient teachers trying to show me how to hold a pen. The pen was supposed to angle toward you and slant toward the right. Easy for you righties, but for lefties like me, it required an unnatural twist of the wrist, a scrunching up of knuckles, and a painful stretch of the thumb. And—worst of all—I couldn't see what I was writing because my clunky, contorted hand was in the way. This was probably a good thing, because when my hand moved on and I finally saw my work product, it wasn't a pretty picture.

Of course, when the teachers weren't looking, I reverted to my more natural stance in which my left arm and hand sat to the west of the target and pushed the pen toward the east. This particular bad habit doomed me to a half-century of ink smeared on my pinky, but at least it didn't hurt *me*; only those who had to try to decipher it.

And it went downhill from there. With college came papers that—bless-edly—had to be typed. (Of course, my typing was no great shakes: two fingers then, same two fingers now). But eventually I reached that level of professional nirvana where all I had to do was dictate.

I thought about all this recently while reading about the new SAT test. Now, instead of merely having to "bubble" the correct answers, aspiring collegians have to write an essay. And they have to do it *by hand*.

Of course, the kind folks at ETS assure these kids that penmanship doesn't count. But these high-octane, overachieving kids, who (with their paranoid über-competitive boomer parents urging them on) seek out every possible edge in the college admission sweepstakes, and who have been taught from birth that *every-thing* on their "permanent record" counts, just don't believe a word of it. So they have been fretting about having to write both brilliantly *and* legibly for about a half hour. [Pardon me, sir, your schaedenfreude is showing.]

So this is one of those rare and delicious moments when it's not so bad to be in one's late 50s, when it is safe to say that penmanship *really* doesn't count. Sure, there are times when I need to write a personal note on a card, but I convince myself that it's the "thought" that counts. And yes, I do have to edit the fruits of my dictation, and I do that by hand—much to the chagrin of those who must make head or tail out of it.

Actually, there is one other time when someone has to read my atrocious handwriting, and I'll give you a hint. These occasional essays got written in odd places, at odd times, which is wherever and whenever an idea flitted into my aging brain. And when it hit, there was no computer, recorder, or even a steno pad in sight; just pen and paper. It's a bit like being back in second grade—but with penmanship that isn't half as good now as it was then.

30

THE WORLD WE JUST MISSED

A few years ago, I had the pleasure of reading David McCullough's biography *Truman*. It was a great read about an endlessly fascinating figure in history.

But for this boomer, it was more. It focused on a period (the Truman presidency, 1945-53) that began a couple of years before I was born and ended around the time I was in kindergarten. Thus, it covered a period that had largely escaped my consciousness of national and world affairs, which didn't really kick in until several years later. I dimly recall the 1956 election, in part because the names on the Democratic ticket seemed so odd: Adlai and Estes. What kind of names were they? It wasn't until the 1960 election, when I was 13, that I really had some idea what was going on, and formed memories that would stay with me.

What I enjoyed so much about *Truman* was that it described a world that I didn't know personally, but which bore intriguing similarities to the world of my earliest memories. For example, it was a world in which radio played a huge role, while black-and-white television was just getting started. Truman's world seemed vaguely familiar, yet still just over the horizon of my memory.

These thoughts came to mind recently when I saw "Good Night and Good Luck," George Clooney's wonderful tribute to Edward R. Murrow, the first great TV journalist. I actually remembered watching Murrow as a kid. He always seemed to be smoking on TV in the 1950s, and Clooney's film—accurately, I suspect—shows the CBS newsroom as more smoke-filled than the clubhouses in which political candidates used to be selected.

Of course, years later, I learned about Murrow's real contribution: taking on Sen. Joseph McCarthy during the height of America's paranoia over communism. This came at a time when most members of the media feared that if they even questioned McCarthy's "facts," they themselves would be branded as communists or at least "fellow travelers." But I appreciated none of this while it actually took place. I was just too young and too incurious. It was part of my world, yet it was a world that I just missed.

This got me thinking about other generations, and the worlds which *they* missed. For example, there are millions of Americans who are well into their 30s, raising families and hitting their stride in their careers, who have no real clue about the Vietnam War. They couldn't possibly remember the early build-up and the "domino theory" that justified it, or the weekly body count, or General Hershey, the Selective Service System, and the "lottery." They might have read about the Cambodian "incursion," or the protests it spawned, or the Kent State shooting that followed, but to them, it's as remote as Woodrow Wilson is to us.

And it helps me understand why my own kids and others born in the 1980s don't have—because they couldn't have—the historical perspective to understand the politics of the 21st century. After all, they not only missed Vietnam; they completely missed Watergate, and—for all practical purposes—they missed the Reagan neo-con "revolution" that gave birth to much of today's politics. It may be possible to understand Iraq without having lived through Vietnam, but it can't be easy. And our kids may look at the White House's alleged dirty tricks in outing a CIA agent, and the cover-up which followed, and scratch their heads. But it's a tad easier to put it in proper perspective when you recall the chain of events which started at the Watergate during the run-up to the "blow-out" 1972 election.

But it does help to go back to visit the worlds we missed. I am sure it was no accident that, in "Good Night and Good Luck," Mr. Clooney shows the eerie similarity between the fear mongers of the 50s and the fear mongers of today, with terrorists having replaced the communists.

What it comes down to is this: history always seems to repeat itself, but we can never be sure if we're living through Act I or Act II.

31

WAR AND PEACE

The year 2005 ushered in considerable blather about members of the post-war Baby Boom generation beginning to turn 60. We were all treated to discussions of how, when and where the boomers will retire; whether and how they will afford it; the steadily increasing demands on our healthcare system; and so forth.

Surprisingly—or perhaps not—there was relatively little talk in 2005 about the event which, after all, was the starting gun for our generation 60 years ago: the end of World War II in August 1945. That's too bad, because a look back at the final months of the war in the Pacific can be a sobering reminder of how far we've all traveled in 60 years—or perhaps not.

In *Flyboys*, author James Bradley tells the story of the incredibly brave pilots and crew members who fought the Japanese on their home turf, including the strategically crucial Japanese islands of Iwo Jima and Chichi Jima. Bradley holds back nothing in describing the carnage wrought over wide swaths of Japanese cities even before Hiroshima and Nagasaki. He describes in painful detail the staggering losses suffered on both sides. He brings to light, in chilling detail, how the starving Japanese troops, whose supply chains had been snapped, resorted to cannibalism with captured American servicemen. In so many ways, Bradley reminds us of how much we owe to the Flyboys, a bunch of talented, brave and (at the time) unbelievably *young* men from around the United States.

But what struck me the most was Bradley's description of the ceremony in Tokyo Bay when, at long last, the Japanese surrendered:

> Both President Truman and General MacArthur addressed the U.S. in a live radio hookup. Like their counterparts in the nineteenth century, they couched their remarks with repeated references to "civilization" and their Christian god. Truman's speech was almost religious in tone. The Japanese were "forces of evil" who had posed a "mighty threat to civilization." It was "God's help" that "brought us to this day of victory" over those who were out to "destroy

His civilization." Truman used the words "God" and "civilized" five times each—as often as he said the word "America."

Sound familiar?

For our generation and those which followed, it is hard today to imagine that we ever fought a war with the country that sends us Toyotas, PlayStations and Hideki Matsui. Hollywood never tires of making movies about the war against Germany in Europe. Remember *The Longest Day*? And how about *Saving Private Ryan*? But why is it that we see and hear much less about the war against Japan? Is it because the war in Europe played out in quaint French and Belgian villages, in contrast to the Pacific Theater, which was—after all—mostly a lot of ocean?

Bradley and his book remind us that in contrast to Germany, which attacked our allies, Japan attacked *us* at Pearl Harbor. He demonstrates how the prewar cultures in Japan and the United States were so irrelevant to each other that they might just as well have existed on different planets. Bradley also pulls no punches in reminding us of the degree to which the war against Japan was fueled by raw racial hatred—in both directions. But Bradley also tells us about the Flyboys (and, yes, their Japanese counterparts) who, during the second half of the 20th century, came to transcend the fervent hatred that once divided the two nations for reasons that now seem increasingly distant and perplexing.

But the story of the *Flyboys* also reminds us that there really is nothing new under the sun. For how many centuries have self-described "civilized" people fought wars against the forces of "evil"? For how many more centuries will it continue after we've gone?

And if there is any doubt that our 60-year-old generation is part of one long continuum, consider the fact that one of the most courageous Flyboys extolled by Bradley for helping win the war in the Pacific was one of the few who survived. That Flyboy went on to another career which included yet another war against another enemy who has perhaps been demonized as much as the Japanese Emperor was 60 years ago.

That Flyboy was George H.W. Bush.

32

TWO SCORE AND TEN YEARS AGO ...

These three things all happened to this boomer in one week early in 2006.

First, while getting a pastrami fix at a certain delicatessen on Houston Street in New York City, I was musing about the fact that this deli had been in business for 118 years. As the cholesterol coursed through my arteries, I realized that I had been patronizing this deli since my parents introduced me to it when I was a little boy. About fifty years ago.

Second, I was invited by an old friend to a celebration of his firm's 25th anniversary. It was fun to meet and chat with his colleagues and clients, none of whom I'd met before. When asked what my own connection to the firm was, I explained that I was so-and-so's oldest friend. And when pressed to explain exactly how long we'd been friends, I replied that we met in third grade. Fifty years ago.

Finally, that same week, I came across an article in the paper which noted sardonically that the "warranty" on the Tappan Zee Bridge had "expired." The article explained that the bridge had been built on the cheap in 1956, and had been projected to last only 50 years. What astonished me was *not* that a government agency had been so short-sighted about what was bound to become, and did become, a crucial link in the transportation system. What *did* astonish me was that I actually remembered the Tappan Zee being first opened. Fifty years ago.

What's going on here?

What's going on is that we early boomers, born in the late 1940s, are reaching a point in life where we have memories that are *50 years old*. We have relationships that have spanned *half a century*.

Of course, it was bound to happen, and I'm sure for some boomers it started before it did for me. I've heard that you just don't remember much, if anything, from your first years of life. But there comes a point in life when memories begin to get hardwired to our brains, and some of those memories hang on for life. For example, I have no memory at all of Harry Truman, who was president for the first five or so years of my life. And I completely missed the Korean War and lots of other stuff in the early 1950s.

But sometime around the mid-1950s, the lasting memories began to form. It will be interesting to see how many of these half-century-old recollections return to our consciousness as we boomers march toward and beyond the Big Six-Oh. You can bet that soon we will routinely be hearing bloviating boomers talking about what happened two score and ten years ago.

Of course, for many of us, there were events that made such a vivid impression that you can't help remembering them for 50 years and even longer. For me, it was a day in late 1956. Adlai Stevenson was campaigning for president and held a rally in my own blue neighborhood within the bluest of blue states. A 40-something woman had a chance to shake Stevenson's hand, and she did so with all her heart and soul. She had a smile on her face that could have lit up the entire city. It was a smile that said something like, *This Is As Good As It Gets*.

A photographer caught that woman and that handshake. The next day, the picture of this woman with Adlai Stevenson appeared in the newspaper.

Now, 50 years later, I have little recollection of Mr. Stevenson. He was defeated—a second time—by Dwight Eisenhower in the fall election, by a wide margin.

I can dimly recall the newspaper. I believe it was the *New York Herald Tribune*. This was at a time when New York had about seven papers, some of which were already amalgams of two or three earlier papers. The *Trib*, at least, survives—but not in this country.

But I still keep a copy of that picture of the woman excitedly shaking Adlai's hand. Though it was a half-century ago, I remember this 50-year-old event like it was yesterday—undoubtedly for this reason:

That woman was my mother.

Boomers @ Home

33

SUBURBAN FLIGHT

Remember when people were writing epitaphs for America's big cities? It was only a few decades ago that our cities were suffering from crime, racial unrest, poverty, drugs, filth—you name it. The middle class was leaving the cities in droves, seeking refuge in the suburbs which ringed every city.

Back then, some believed that even the suburbs were too close for comfort. We were hearing about people moving to the "exurbs"—the very distant once-rural areas beyond the 'burbs. There seemed to be no limit to how far away from cities people might move, other than the fact that if you moved too far out of some cities (*e.g.*, Baltimore) in certain directions (*e.g.*, northeast), you could back into the suburbs of another city (*e.g.*, Philadelphia) or even—perish the thought!—another actual city.

Some of us boomers went along for the ride as our parents began the first big wave of movement away from the cities. Other boomers led the way to new and more distant suburbs in which to build McMansions or at least find an affordable, safe place to live. As business and industry followed people out of urban centers, many of us found that our lives were more and more disconnected from big cities.

Given that history, one might have expected our children to push even further outward, exploring places unknown. After all, this is still a huge country, with sparsely populated states that are bigger in area than some European nations. Surely, by now, we would see young people working in the far distant suburbs of Chicago (say, central Iowa) and living somewhere even further out (say, Montana).

But a funny thing happened to a lot of children of baby boomers. After spending their adolescence being bored to tears by the suburbs, they used college as an opportunity to escape—to a big city. And this trickle of young people into our cities seems to have become a torrent as our kids have graduated college and entered the work force. It seems like every young man and woman in their 20s that I meet wants to work and live in a city, the bigger city the better, and—if at all possible—New York. Our kids are becoming totally urban creatures. There seems to be an excitement about urban life today among our children which hasn't been seen since the heyday of our grandparents.

Oh—and one more thing. Some baby boomers—ever anxious to climb on a good bandwagon—are following their kids back into the cities. With a little more money than they had 20 years ago, and the responsibilities of childrearing behind them, they are trading their suburban digs for places that are smaller, noisier and more expensive, giving up strip malls for theaters, museums, restaurants, ethnic neighborhoods—the whole shooting match that we and/or our parents escaped, for reasons that are now getting harder and harder to remember.

I could be wrong, but I don't hear a lot of boomers talking about retiring to Florida, Arizona or the other places earlier generations went. But sooner or later, the boomers *will* retire, and they're likely to go somewhere—*anywhere*—to escape the boring suburbs.

I have a sneaking suspicion that in five or ten years, much of what is left of our supersized generation, which overcrowded colleges and the work force for so long, is going to start overrunning places like the East Side of Manhattan, Lakeshore Drive, Beacon Hill, Rittenhouse Square and Georgetown. If our kids continue to have no interest in moving near us in the 'burbs once they become parents, boomer grandparents may start moving into the cities to be near their grandchildren. This suburban flight will probably bid up the cost of housing in our cities so much that future generations will be forced to seek out cheaper housing wherever it can be found—which is to say, the suburbs that we will be deserting.

And a lot of us boomers will just say what we've always said: better them than us.

34

BOOMERS OF A FEATHER

As a service to our readers, we today offer a field guide to the unusual nesting habits of the different species that form the genus known as *Boomerus*. By studying these nesting characteristics, you should be able to identify a species simply by studying its habitat.

- *Boomerus contractus*. Member of this species shed their large nests when their young get their wings and leave home for college, employment, or mating. Prior to downsizing into smaller nests, this species molts by shedding unnecessary baggage, often at a garage sale. Offspring who show up at these garage sales to protect their belongings risk having a price tag placed on their foreheads.

- *Boomerus boomerangus*. This species starts out like its close relative, *Boomerus contractus*, but much like salmon which return to where they were born, the offspring of this species is attracted back to the downsized nest, usually when the offspring run out of work, money and foodstuffs. The nests of *Boomerus boomerangus* are characterized by beds in the attic or basement, unwashed clothes in the laundry room, and empty refrigerators. Legends suggesting that this species eats its young have never been confirmed.

- *Boomerus expansus*. In this unusual species, after the young leave the nest, instead of evolving into *Boomerus contractus*, this species undergoes an odd genetic mutation, causing it to *upsize* its nest. Unlike its cousin *Boomerus contractus*, this species actually tries to lure its young back to the parents' nest. The offspring of this species often cannot find the new nest, and occasionally stop trying, in order to avoid pressure from their parents to mate and procreate. The acoustics in these nests are highly unusual, believed to be a result of echoes resonating through empty rooms.

- *Boomerus snowbirdus*. This species has not one nest, but two, usually in different climates many miles apart. Their migratory patterns are as well established as they are bizarre, often involving extensive flying hither and yon during the period when the temperate nest is occupied, in order to accumulate frequent flier mileage needed to enable flight to the tropical nest.

- *Boomerus triresidus*. This rare species has *three* nests, with the third nest in a climate contrarily selected for its likelihood to be snow covered for months at a time. Due to difficulties in traveling to, from and around the arctic nest, this species will often acquire a motor vehicle that is just slightly smaller than a diesel locomotive. Postmortem tests conducted on some member of this species have revealed an unusually large number of limbs that are both fractured and sunburned.

- *Boomerus immovabilis*. This species, found only in certain urban centers, occupies a nest which features the rare but highly sought after trait known as rent control. Members of this hardy species protect their nests so tenaciously that they have been known to migrate daily to employment in different time zones, returning to the nest every evening. The urge to procreate in this species is unusually pronounced, owing to an instinctive need to continue saving money on rent long after death.

- *Boomerus fixupus*. Members of this fascinating species select their nests by—believe it or not—seeking out the most ramshackle place they can find, tearing down much of the existing infrastructure, and replacing it with new materials chosen to look as old as possible. This species has been spotted in a bewildering array of different locales, but a high percentage of this species is located within a half hour of a Home Depot.

- *Boomerus winnebagus*. This nomadic species has no fixed nest. Rather, it lives in a large enclosure which has four wheels (plus a spare) and an internal combustion engine—sort of a McMansion with power steering. The engine and wheels protect this species from becoming a *Boomerus boomerangus*: when the offspring head home, the parents spring off. This species is especially adept at avoiding the resident income tax imposed by many states: no discernible income and no residence. Some members of this species keep count of the number of states visited. A small, overachieving group of them are waiting for the globe to warm up enough for them to drive to Hawaii.

35

LET'S PLAY JEOPARDY

I recently read an article in *USA Today* (it came with a hotel room—honest!) about making homes safer for aging baby boomers. It illustrated (in full color, of course) the numerous danger spots in a typical home, and described how to retrofit them to protect fragile boomers. For example, it advocated turning down the temperature of your hot water heater to prevent scalding; installing grab bars near tubs; moving high-up microwaves to countertop level; and the like.

Putting aside the more nauseating and condescending aspects of the article, *i.e.*, how pathetic we must now seem to younger generations, I think the article missed the boat. A typical home has all kinds of not-so-obvious traps for vulnerable boomers that this article failed to address. Let's take a tour through some of the *really* dangerous spots in a 21st century boomer home.

Let's start with that "security system" with the keypad near the front door. You need to key in a four-digit code—and do it *quickly*—unless you want the system to go off. And if it does go off, you'll have to give a secret password, or else the police will show up. Do they honestly expect people our age to remember a four-digit code *and* a password? Get real.

Then there's that Tivo® or DVR wired to your favorite TV. Let's assume your kids or some other tech-savvy person got the system up and running for you. Now you're recording every episode of every show you never really bothered to watch. So what's the problem? Keep it up, fellow boomers, and the time needed to watch all your accumulated shows will exceed your steadily diminishing life expectancy.

Or take something as seemingly safe and innocuous as your refrigerator. But open that big box, and you might find—food! And not just carrots and broccoli, but leftover brisket and butter-laden premium ice cream. And if you don't think *that* stuff is dangerous, call your cardiologist—*STAT!*

Of course, every house is likely to have mirrors—perhaps several of them. Are we concerned that they may break, and that we'll get cut by shards of glass? Of course not. The big risk is that they *won't* break, and that we'll actually see ourselves. And these are not those trick mirrors they have in some clothing stores that make you look 20 pounds thinner. These are the real deal, and what you'll see is the real you. Avoid these like the plague.

And let's not forget the garage. Don't go there, because if you do, and in the unlikely event that you can find your car keys, you might get into a car and drive away. So are we concerned that hapless boomers will drive too fast? Of course not. At our age, we're getting to that point that we drive too *slow*. And why is that a problem? The apoplectic drivers behind us—who, of course, are at least 30 years younger—will start blasting their horns at us. And if we react the same way as old-timers from earlier generations, we will be rewarded the same way they were: by the shouting of expletives and the flipping of the bird as they roar by us on the right.

Yet another danger spot in boomer homes is the home office with that home computer. Like every other thoroughly modern boomer, you've learned how to check your office e-mail from home. Aren't you modern and tech-savvy? You can be connected to work any time, day or night! And this has lulled you into believing you can work any "flex time" you want. Feel like a round of golf in the middle of a work day? Go for it! You can check your e-mail when you get home.

So what's the danger? Well, suppose you log on to your e-mail and discover a company-wide message offering every employee a dream buyout before the jobs are off-shored to central Asia. The only catch is that you had to hand in your signed papers in person by the unextendable deadline.

Which came and went two hours ago.

Food For
Boomer Thought

36

DON'T MISS THAT EARLY BIRD SPECIAL

Having once been young ourselves (for quite a few decades, actually), we early boomers who are approaching 60 are painfully aware of what happens to folks when they begin to enter codgerdom. After all, we first saw it play out in our grandparents and, later, we saw it as our parents got older.

We're talking here about those idiosyncrasies that seem to be so pronounced among older people. You know what I mean: a tendency to fixate on minor things; an overdeveloped devotion to routine; perhaps a slight touch of narcissistic self-indulgence; and all the rest.

Of course, we have experienced all of this as spectators. But perhaps it is not too early to raise this troublesome question: are we boomers reaching that point ourselves? You be the judge.

A recent personal experience brings these questions to mind. At the organization in which I work, there are routine senior staff meetings about every two weeks. They are boring; they are repetitive; they are usually unproductive; they are always scheduled for lunchtime; and they always take place on Thursdays. This routine has been engraved in stone for a number of years.

But recently, when the schedule for the next round of these Thursday lunch meetings was circulated, certain unidentified attendees raised an objection. With little fanfare, to the surprise of some, this resulted in all of the meetings being shifted to Tuesdays.

What was the reason? Did it have anything to do with travel schedules? Did some hotshot routinely start long weekends early? Did the Thursday meetings conflict with some other professional commitments? Was there some other business-related reason for the change?

The answers: no, no, no, and no. So what *was* the reason?

Split pea soup.

You know what I'm talking about here. That thick, plebian *potage* with those tangy, garlicky croutons (carbs be damned). Comfort food in a cup or—better yet—in a bowl.

An investigation into the mysterious change of the meeting schedule quickly revealed that a few senior people of the boomer persuasion are huge fans of split pea soup. In fairness, it would be more accurate to say that they seem to be obsessed with the stuff. They are willing to rearrange schedules to make sure they get their ration of split pea soup; and whenever possible, they plan their schedules around it in the first place.

In the interest of full disclosure, I must confess that I am one of them.

So what's the problem? Well, it turns out that in the area in which I work, in diners and various other eateries, split pea is the "soup of the day" on Thursdays. This practice seems so universal that I sometimes wonder if split pea soup on Thursdays is mandated by state law.

It was thus revealed that this little cabal of aging boomers had been suffering for years with these biweekly lunch meetings taking place on Thursdays. If every meeting took place as scheduled, we would miss out on half our annual allocation of split pea soup. Our group would secretly hope that some of these meetings would get canceled, *not* because they are boring, repetitive, and wasteful (as indeed they are), but because it would give us an unexpected opportunity to run out for split pea soup at lunchtime.

Which brings us back to the question: have we gone over the edge into eccentric codgerdom? I suspect that some of the younger turks in our organization believe we have. (Actually, they're probably sure of it.) Is this little bit of quirkiness on a par with earlier generations in Florida planning their day around getting out for dinner in time for the early bird special? As I said, you be the judge.

Organizations being what they are, those senior staff meetings at our place will make the initially uncomfortable shift to Tuesdays, but eventually it will settle in as the new routine. Sooner or later, our little group of soup-obsessed boomers will pass from the scene, and eventually no one will be left who remembers exactly how it came to pass that these meetings always take place on Tuesdays.

No one—that is—but you.

37

TO GO

I would never be so bold as to suggest that the baby boom generation actually *invented* takeout food. I am certain that if one digs deep into the history of takeout, one would find an occasional hot dog wrapped in wax paper leaving some local deli prior to the Truman administration. Heck, you might even find that some early 19th century president had Maryland crab cakes (with tartar sauce, of course) smuggled into the White House.

But I don't think I'm sticking my neck out by suggesting that takeout came of age with our generation.

I remember being a teenager when my parents discovered a wonderful little Italian place several blocks from our apartment. The food was great, particularly those veal parmigiana heroes. But the place was so tiny as to be claustrophobic.

So on one fateful day, necessity being then (as always) the mother of invention, we discovered that we could order those blissful sandwiches *to go*, and eat them in the comfort of home. But this created a logistical dilemma. The place was maybe a half-mile away, a distance that could be covered in two minutes or less in the family car. But where I grew up, a convenient parking space was so precious that you had to be nuts to give it up just to go pick up takeout; for when you got back home, you might have to cruise the neighborhood for an hour looking for another spot.

So the preferred mode of travel was on foot: slower but reliable. If I kept up a good pace, and if the traffic lights didn't gang up on me, I could stride in with the heroes while they were still warm and wonderful. Thus was I introduced to the "takeout trot," an early form of power walking characterized by the parcel being carried by the walker emitting steam and sporting a growing grease stain. To this day, when I'm driving, I always honor that crucial rule of the road: Yield To Pedestrian Carrying Pizza Box.

In the decades since, it has become possible to take out virtually any form of prepared food from any cuisine. And before long, the eateries took over the job of getting the food from their kitchens to our dining rooms. Pick up the phone, and moo shu pork can be coming through your front door in 20 minutes.

Much has been said and written about this phenomenon. We're told that it resulted from families with two parents working outside the home, with no time to cook, but retaining a desire for the family to come together for a meal. Others say that no one can replicate in his or her own kitchen all the delicious cuisines that are out there today. Still others say that all of us boomers have just gotten too lazy to cook, and *much* too lazy to clean pots and pans.

But there has to be more to the appeal of takeout. After all, the food must taste better at the restaurant. It's gotta be hotter, and it's bound to look a heckuva lot more appealing at your local bistro than it does in a foil pan with a cardboard cover.

I could be wrong, but I think I have a clue why some boomers—like me—would rather chow down at home. When you eat out, you usually have to dress like a housebroken grown-up. That often means pants that are barely big enough to put on even in the morning, held up by a belt that's already on its last hole. As we scarf up that last spoonful of food at the local restaurant, our busting gut has nowhere to go.

But take that dinner home and—*voila!* While the food is cooling off in the kitchen, it's into the bedroom, where off comes the lower body straightjacket and on come the blessed sweatpants—preferably the ones with the elastic waistband that will forgive your every culinary indiscretion.

While you mull that over, if you're thinking of getting a bite to eat, I'll take a General Tso's chicken and a small order of fried rice....

38

ONE CUPPA JOE, HOLD THE PRETENSE

The determination of the baby boom generation to complicate nearly everything is perhaps best illustrated by what has happened to the simple and innocent cup of coffee under our watch. My own personal journey through a half-century of coffee may show you what I mean.

As a youngster, I learned that coffee was a mostly adult pleasure that I'd learn about soon enough. My mother drank half a dozen cups of black coffee a day, and insisted that she couldn't fall asleep unless she had one final cup while enjoying Jack Paar on TV. It took me years to realize how perplexing this was, since this was the era *before* decaf became readily available.

When I went off to college, my roommate showed up with a kit for making coffee in our dorm room: a jar of instant, powdered Coffeemate, sugar packets, and a plug-in heater to boil the water, which carried a lifetime guarantee that it would short out any electrical system that did or didn't meet the building code.

It was part of the culture at my college that freshmen had to pull all-nighters before big exams, fueled by strong coffee. I tried it once and managed to stay awake 'til about 6 AM, when either the caffeine or my central nervous system gave up the ghost. What I looked like when the alarm went off an hour later was not a pretty picture, nor was my grade on that exam.

As years and then decades flew by, my coffee habit went through gradual changes. During one of my periodic intense but invariably short-lived diets, I shed the milk and sugar from my coffee; and while the weight always returned, the milk and sugar didn't, moving me into that select circle of coffee addicts who take it straight up. (Mom would be proud.) Later, when young children entered my life, staying awake ceased to be a problem. I began my dalliances with decaf, but sooner or later I always pulled up my mug to the high-test pump.

As luck would have it, I was sort of present at the creation of a new era of coffee. My one visit to Seattle took place at a time when Starbucks and Seattle's Best were battling it out on nearly every corner of the Pacific Northwest, but hadn't yet exploded into a national phenomenon. They served great coffee in cool shops, but (demonstrating an uncanny ability to miss the boat that would serve me well for decades) I couldn't imagine there being enough coffee drinkers for it all to make sense.

Which brings me to the 21st century. Still enjoying a good cup of coffee in the morning, I stop at Starbuck's on the way to the office, where I truly become a stranger in a strange land. They speak a tongue there that is foreign to me. As I wait to be served, the customers in front of me in line—a few of whom are even fellow boomers—rattle off orders that are incomprehensible to me. Some of the individual words sound familiar: "half," "iced," "mocha," "caramel," "shot," "soy," etc., but it all happens so fast that I cannot imagine what the final product is supposed to be. But I do get some idea when I see customers heading out with their "beverages," which to me look suspiciously like sundaes from Dairy Queen.

When I get to the front of the line, it is now the moment of truth. I just want a large cup of coffee, but the fear of being outed as a dinosaur gets the most of me. I have at least learned to say "venti" when I really mean "large." And in a pathetic quest to seem as quirkily individualistic as everyone else, this boomer eschews the regular funnel-shaped lid, which reliably sprays coffee on my pants as it sits in my car's cup holder for the two-minute ride to the office, in favor of the retro "flat top," which merely allows hot droplets of Breakfast Blend to ooze out the edges onto my hand as I go from the car to my desk.

Isn't keeping up with the times cool?

*Caution: Boomers
At Work (Or Not)*

39

EXPERIENCE THIS

The first time most baby boomers learned about "experience" was when we applied for a job, found out that experience was something we didn't have, and were told that we should come back when we had some.

Actually, that wasn't really our very first brush with experience. Remember how, during adolescence, we would marvel at someone—usually of the opposite sex—whose level of sexual advancement surpassed our own? We described such people as "experienced." But we won't go *there* today.

I believe my very first encounter with "experience" was playing a '50s-vintage board game called "Careers." As you met certain challenges, you were rewarded with "Experience Cards." They were simply cards with numbers like 1, 2 or 3. You could use them to plan out your moves, instead of depending on the vagaries of rolling the dice. If a particularly good opportunity was one square away, you could play a "1" Experience Card and assure yourself of landing on that magical square. Or, if big trouble lay two squares in front of you, you could play a "3" and safely skip over it.

But let's go back to those unsettling days when we couldn't get a job because we had no experience. It sometimes seemed as though the entire American workforce would grow old and die, taking with them vast amounts of experience, while we baby boomers would remain on the sidelines forever, doomed to perpetual unemployment because no one would hire us without experience, and because we couldn't get that first hunk of experience because no one would hire us.

But somehow we got past that stage. Now, three decades or so later, we are the old pros—the veterans who have seen and done it all, the people in our organizations who are looked at as the ones with all those years of "experience." When our younger colleagues or family members ask us if we've ever run into a certain type of situation, the answer is often yes.

As it turns out, the game "Careers" wasn't all that far off the mark. No, we didn't accumulate little cards that we could play out with surgical precision. But it is true that each new project, case, patient, sales target or whatever taught us a few lessons. It also seems that we accumulated the most experience points when we hit a patch of bad luck or, even more so, when we just plain screwed up. And as we progressed through adulthood, it seemed to get a little easier to spot the opportunities and seize them, and to spot those minefields and navigate around them. Kind of like playing those "1," "2" and "3" space Experience Cards.

But it also seems that experience has its limits. There are those in our generation who have accumulated experience, yet they still roll the dice when they could play an "Experience Card" instead. There are special names for people like that—in fact, there are two: "homeless people" and "billionaires."

But for that vast majority of baby boomers who prefer their risks in small doses, experience is something we draw on daily. We often try to pass it on to our children, but it doesn't work now, just as it didn't work when we were their age. Experience is one form of wealth that—for the most part—can't be passed from one generation to another. We can't give it away in life or in death.

I am finding of late that there is one more limitation on experience that I hadn't bargained for: our increasing loss of memory. We're not just forgetting names, events, facts and figures. We're also forgetting some of those good moves we made in the past and—yes—some of those screw-ups as well. I suspect our generation is now just about straddling that point where our experience is at its maximum, but the ability to draw upon it is beginning to diminish.

Perhaps the sweetest thing now about accumulating experience is this: our disappointments don't hurt quite so much, since we've been there before; but when people our age pull out a victory, it feels better than ever.

40

THE OTHER FOOT

I realize this all happened a long time ago, but do you boomers remember when you were just starting out? Do you recall those painful days when you were applying for entry level positions?

You must remember that it was painful beyond belief. We would sit there on the wrong side of a large desk, having no experience to offer and not much else. We would dress up in neat business attire, just like our interviewers, and try to act mature beyond our years and free of the influence of any illicit substances.

The person on the good side of the desk was in total control of the situation. Everything about that person smacked of total competence, encyclopedic knowledge of the business, and complete freedom from fear. As we sat there groping for the best answer to each question, the interviewer might make or take a phone call to order around some subordinate, or might casually joke around with another, equally intimidating, colleague, or lead us around the place because they knew exactly where everything and everyone was, while we were beyond clueless.

Surely you must have had some pangs of jealousy during that painful process. I certainly did. I couldn't imagine ever being on the other side of the interviewing process. How sweet it would be—I remember thinking—to have control of the situation, and to sit in judgment while someone much younger and much less experienced practically begged for acceptance.

Fast forward by about 30 years or so. Perhaps you, like me and other boomers, find yourself in a position where you have responsibility for hiring young people. Today, we are the ones who sit behind big desks which—unlike the ones we gawked at back in the 60s and 70s—are cluttered with computers and other high-tech gizmos that only some of us know how to use. *We* are suddenly the ones who get to sit in judgment of young ambitious people and carefully select the best and the brightest. *We* are the ones who are now in control of making the decision whether to make an offer or not.

This was supposed to be easy, right? Well, I for one find that it is anything but a cakewalk.

I sometimes have to screen big piles of résumés of young people seeking to get started in my field. I am constantly astonished at how accomplished all these young people seem to be, at least on paper. In addition to degrees and summer jobs, it seems like every young person today has had one or two impressive sounding internships or externships, or some other kind of "-ternships" that I never knew existed. It often seems impossible to pluck a few out of the pile while passing on the rest.

And then comes the interviewing process. Aside from the occasional budding sociopath, almost every young applicant I meet seems one heck of a lot more impressive than I remember myself being at that age. They wear the same sober business attire applicants have always worn, while we sit there adorned in "business casual." I often think they *all* deserve to be hired, but people in our situations get paid to make careful, astute and hard decisions.

Sitting on the "right" side of the big desk was never a picnic for me. But it has gotten even harder of late as my own children reach the point of sitting in the applicant's seat and hoping to be recognized and hired. I sometimes think that every young person I have to turn down is not all that different from my own kids. And I rue the fact that every résumé that I put in the "do not interview" pile is the son or daughter of some boomer just like me, and that I may be disappointing an entire family. And as I sit in interviews and make those hard decisions about who should or should not be hired, I picture my own kids sitting there, and I worry that some innocuous comment or gesture they make at some interview will sour some boomer interviewer and lead to a rejection letter.

This was supposed to be fun. Surprise! It's not. The shoe is now on the other foot.

And it hurts.

41

THE "R" WORD

Do you remember KFC before it slimmed down to just those three letters? Once upon a time it was called Kentucky Fried Chicken; but the boomer-driven cholesterol police pronounced everything fried to be taboo, so all that remains today is fat-free KFC.

I suspect a similar phenomenon is going on with the AARP, the organization that beckons everyone when they turn 50, much like the Selective Service System sent greetings to male boomers when we turned 18. In the case of the AARP, I have a sneaking suspicion that its initials will come to predominate over the full name—all because of the dreaded "R" word.

Retirement. There, I've said it. As the first wave of boomers started pushing 60, retirement became an issue we will be discussing a great deal for many years to come. And, as with so many other things involving the postwar generation, nothing is simple.

In generations past, retirement seemed to be the prize which everyone sought to earn. If your health was reasonably good and you could afford it, once you turned 65, you could spend your "golden years" in Florida or someplace like it, playing lots of golf, and facing no problem weightier than deciding where and when to eat dinner. And if you had really worked hard, scrimped and saved, you were rewarded by moving your retirement up to age 60, or 55, or even earlier.

I could be wrong, but I think there are vast numbers of boomers for whom the scenario I just described is a vision of hell. No, I'm not talking about our unfortunate compatriots whose 401(k)s have been decimated by huge drops in the stock market or unexpected and protracted runs of involuntary unemployment. Nor am I referring to those boomers who had children late in life, and who are just now contemplating college tuition bills. I'm talking about boomers who could afford to retire today, but would sooner die.

How did *this* strange turn of events come to pass? For many boomers, one of our first heroes was Dobie Gillis' beatnik friend Maynard G. Krebs, whose attitude toward entering the labor force was summed up by that rhetorical sentence consisting of one four-letter word: "*Work?!?!*" How could it be that so many boomers who (to put it mildly) didn't seem all that anxious to knock themselves out back around the 1960s, now seem ambivalent about—if not completely against—retirement?

There are plenty of explanations to go around, but I think it has a lot to do with the kind of work we boomers ended up doing, compared with that of earlier generations. Our grandparents and our parents—particularly those who came of age during the Great Depression—had to take whatever work they could find. They may have been bored by their work, and even may have hated it, but they worked as long as they had to in order to raise and educate their children—meaning us—and gave it up at the first opportunity.

Many boomers, on the other hand, had the luxury of seeking out "meaningful" work, which often meant college, perhaps some graduate school, and maybe even a false start or two. We sometimes weren't sure what it was we wanted to do, but what we *didn't* want to do was fall into the same trap as earlier generations.

And so, what seems to have happened is this: many members of our generation who struggled so hard to "find themselves" actually did. And thirty-something years later, we actually still like what we do, and because of that, we've gotten pretty good at it, too. These boomers would no sooner give up their careers abruptly than they would give up coffee, sex or other pleasurable stimulants.

Sure, many boomers were not as lucky. They will retire when they can; and some will start second careers that are more fulfilling than their first. But a lot of boomers are going to hang in there—perhaps with a reduced workload—until they are carried out. And, strange though it may seem, with all these educated, motivated and now highly experience boomers still at it, the greatest accomplishments of our generation may still be in the future.

The Boomer
Body Politic

42

SAVE SOCIAL SECURITY: HERE'S HOW

The genius behind Social Security is, of course, what threatens to be its downfall. Workers have F.I.C.A. taxes withheld and put into their "accounts," and when they retire, they make what appear to be withdrawals from those "accounts." The reality, of course, is that payments to retirees are funded by current F.I.C.A. taxes paid by the active (*i.e.*, younger) workforce.

To be sure, we've all heard that the baby boom generation threatens to screw the whole system up. There are too many boomers heading toward retirement and too few workers from later generations to fund the payouts to boomers. How do we save Social Security?

Fortunately, some boomer tax policy wonks have come up with creative ways to enhance federal revenues. Best of all, they all appear on their face to spread the burden equitably across all generations. The good news for boomers is that, in reality, the lion's share of the cost will be fobbed off on other generations. Here's a sneak preview:

• *The Text Message Excise Tax.* You know those phones we all carry in our pockets these days? Well, you can do more with them than just talk. You can actually "type" messages and send them to your friends, who can read them on the phone's "screen" and respond in kind. The tax will be a nickel for each call, plus a surcharge based on a complicated formula that uses the value each letter takes in SCRABBLE. (No surcharge for numbers, punctuation marks or blank spaces!) Sure, boomers could send text messages if they want, and pay a share of this tax. But what boomer today has eyesight good enough to type and read those microscopic messages?

• *The Body Jewelry Personal Property Tax.* This tax will be levied on all metallic articles that pierce human skin. The tax will be based on the weight and purity of the article and will be higher where the article is visible on one wearing normal clothes, such that bellybutton piercings enjoy a healthy discount over nose rings. To make the tax really fair to boomers, there will be an Equitable Ear Exemption to assure that no tax is payable on anyone's first two ear piercings. Congress can pass this tax as part of a package with ...

- *The Toot Sweet Tattoo Tax.* This tax is as simple as the tattoo procedure itself: two dollars per square inch. All military personnel of all ages are exempt, provided they served before 1975.

- *The Downright Fair Downloading Tax.* Why fight the desire of so many people (mostly younger, by sheer happenstance) to download and copy music? Don't fight it; tax the heck out of it, and kick a small percentage back to the artists who get ripped off. The basis tax is a dime a song, but to encourage greater theft of music that is more "classic" (*i.e.*, created by boomer artists), there will be a surtax on all downloaded music created after 1985.

- *The Big Levy On Gossip (BLOG) Tax.* Surely by now most boomers have heard of BLOGS. Short for "weblogs," they're a kind of personal Web site where the proprietors (mostly under 30, as it just so happens) set forth their musings, and everyone who's interested (a group which includes an infinitesimally small number of boomers) can drop in to read the latest. Well, talk is cheap, but BLOGS no longer are: a buck a day to maintain a BLOG, and a quarter for each visitor.

- *The Unreal Reality TV Tax.* Low-budget "reality" TV shows are a boon to producers, since they cost so little to produce. (We'll resist the urge to interject here that you get what you pay for.) The genius behind this new tax is that it is based on the difference between the cost of producing the "reality" show and the cost of a "benchmark" show (say, an episode of "West Wing"). The cheaper the show is to produce, the higher the tax. And what if the reality TV producers try to pass the tax along to their sponsors? Perfect! They only care about selling products to the 18 to 35 crowd anyway. And guess what generation won't be hurt by *that*.

43

TICK TOCK

A good ol' boy from Texas is in The White House. His party controls both houses of Congress. The party has such a stranglehold on the entire federal government that even the Supreme Court includes a White House crony and enough other justices who share his philosophy as to constitute a working majority.

Sounds like life in these United States around 2002-05, no?

Try 1965.

The Texan in The White House was a Democrat, Lyndon B. Johnson. The Democrats controlled both Houses of Congress, allowing LBJ to ram through all the Democratic initiatives that John Kennedy had only talked about. The White House crony on the Supreme Court was LBJ's friend, Abe Fortas, and his colleagues (Chief Justice Warren and Justices Douglas, Black and Brennan) formed a working majority that usually took the Democratic or "liberal" view on important cases.

Like many boomers, I remember those Kennedy/Johnson years well. The baby boom generation was just starting to become politically aware. We weren't old enough to vote then, but that would come soon enough.

I also remember a valuable lesson that I learned around that time. I was having Sunday dinner with a friend and his family. In the course of a conversation about current events, I remarked that the country seemed to be so thoroughly and irretrievably Democratic that it was hard to imagine power ever going over to the Republicans.

My friend's father leaned back, smiled at my youthful naiveté, and proceeded to explain how politics historically swings back and forth like a pendulum. He told us that no matter how strong one party or political view might seem at any given moment, things always tend to swing back toward the center and beyond. As he also explained, the swing back may be caused by the arrogance and abuses of the party in power, or perhaps just by stagnation and the need for change.

Finally, he explained that the time between swings of the political pendulum can vary, but the swings themselves are inevitable.

Boy, was he ever right. Within a few years after my remark about the hegemony of the Democrats, Richard Nixon was President, and he was reelected in 1972 by such a landslide that it began to appear that the Republicans would control The White House forever. But then along came Watergate and—tick tock—the pendulum swung back to the Democrats in the form of Jimmy Carter. Then—tick tock—it swung right again into the Reagan/Bush I years, and 12 years later—tick tock—it swung left into the Clinton era. (It remains debatable whether the pendulum really swung right again in 2000. That extremely close election suggests that the pendulum was stuck in the middle, not knowing which way to swing.)

The baby boom generation has thus seen the pendulum swing back and forth any number of times since we came of political age in the 1960s. And that is why we should swallow any period of one-party dominance with a grain of salt.

Yes, today there is a Republican from Texas in The White House and, yes, the Republicans had solid control over both Houses of Congress for a number of years. And yes, we have Dick Cheney's hunting buddy, Nino Scalia, leading a conservative Republican claque on the Supreme Court. Today, Republican power relies heavily on its stranglehold over the South. But remember that the South was once solidly *Democratic*. Ironically, by 1965, the Republicans had already made major inroads in the South, with Barry Goldwater winning five Southern states in what was otherwise a Democratic landslide.

We boomers ought to realize by now that it was never a question of *whether* the pendulum will swing back. The real questions were *when* and by how much. By the time the 2006 midterm election was over, we had our answer.

Interestingly, it is often observed that older citizens are more likely to vote than younger ones. Well, *we* are now older, and there are an awful lot of us. *We* may now decide which way the pendulum swings the next time.

I say, let's do it.

44

THE MORE THINGS CHANGE …

The carnage caused by Hurricane Katrina, and the suffering and dislocation left in its wake, affected baby boomers as much as everyone else. Like people younger and older, throughout America and beyond, boomers reacted with compassion and generosity for the victims and anger toward those who might have done more to minimize the destruction and loss.

But for members of the baby boom generation, there was something more. You could describe it as the sort of world-weariness one often associated with those who are old and those who merely think they are. It is an attitude that manifests itself in expressions like "same old, same old," or "the more things change, the more they stay the same."

No, I'm not suggesting that there was anything ordinary about Katrina. On the contrary, the scope of the destruction was mind-boggling. The number of people who were driven from their homes and beyond the borders of their city, their state and even their region—perhaps never to return—is heart-wrenching.

What I *do* mean is that as they approached their 60th year, prior to Katrina, boomers had already seen plenty of death and destruction. To begin with, while we were born after World War II, we grew up surrounded by the memory of the tens of millions of deaths and the horrific destruction caused by "The War" which shaped our generation's entire world.

In the decades that followed, we lived through other wars, floods, earthquakes, famines, and epidemics. And through all these disasters, there were always three constants. One constant, of course, was the horror of injuries, loss, death and destruction. It is always the same: shock, followed by sympathy and concern.

The second constant has always been the generosity and kindness of those who spring into action when these horrible events take place. Katrina was no exception. It always makes you think—if only for one sweet moment—that maybe mankind really is one big family, and we're really all in this together. Heck, this Blue State resident, who is no fan of politicians from the Lone Star State, was bowled over by the extent to which Texans (like so many other Americans and foreigners) opened their hearts, their cities, their homes, and their wallets to the people displaced by Katrina.

The third constant is the failures of humans—and governments made up of humans—who are inevitably held responsible, fairly or otherwise, if not for the disaster itself, then at least for the degree of destruction. Of course, only some disasters, like certain wars, are completely avoidable. Other disasters, like certain epidemics, could be avoided or mitigated with better health care and education. And then there are the natural disasters like Katrina. No human being and no government could have prevented it, but we will spend years debating who should have done what to minimize the risks. And while we fight this last war, new disasters will loom in the future, and they *will* surprise us, one way or the other.

But there is yet another aspect of Katrina that hit home to this baby boomer. The poverty that was exposed by Katrina was a sickening wake-up call, reminding us that much of America remains a third-world country. And the burden of poverty is *still* borne disproportionately by minorities.

It made me think back over 40 years to the 1960s. Lyndon Johnson had assumed the presidency, after the assassination of John F. Kennedy had brought America together to a degree that would not be seen again until September 11, 2001. The struggle for civil rights was making progress, little by little. And on January 8, 1964, in his first State of the Union address, President Johnson told a country still shaken by the events of November 1963, "This administration today, here and now, declares unconditional war on poverty in America."

But before the decade was out, Johnson was undone by the Vietnam War, and before long the war on poverty slipped out of our national consciousness.

And so it is that Hurricane Katrina conclusively answered one more question, at least for this boomer: whatever happened to the war on poverty?

Now we know.

Poverty won.

Culture, Boomer Style

45

ALPHA, DELTA AND OMEGA MALES

What movie best defines the baby boom generation?

Was it, perhaps, *The Graduate*? Or was it one of the other great films that our generation watched in its salad days?—from *Davy Crockett* to *Midnight Cowboy* to the original *Godfather*?

I could be wrong, but I think the winner is a movie that appears on no politically or artistically correct list of great films from that era. It was a low-budget affair, but it struck a chord among at least a significant sector of at least the male half of our generation—a chord that still resonates today.

That movie is *Animal House*.

That's right—the one about the warring fraternities at dear old Faber College. The "Deltas"—Otter, Boone, D-Day and of course Bluto (who would later become a U.S. Senator)—were those guys who partied continuously, passed few if any courses, and ultimately were thrown off campus and into the maw of their draft boards. The "Omegas" were the serious guys—like Greg and Dougie (who would later be killed by his own troops in Vietnam)—who were enlisted by Dean Wormer to help rid Faber of the Deltas.

I used to think that a love for *Animal House* was a character flaw I shared only with a bunch of close male friends. But I began to realize that this was bigger than I had appreciated a few years ago at an NHL playoff game. After the second period, during which the home team had been pounded out of contention with a barrage of goals, the crowd surged toward the rest rooms. The men's room was silent with the deathly smell of elimination (from the playoffs, that is). But from the back of one line—a line with lots of boys and men who weren't even alive when *Animal House* was released—a lone voice sounded the call made famous by Brother Bluto after Delta was finally kicked off campus, and one of the Deltas suggested that the party was over: "Was it over when the Germans bombed Pearl Harbor?"

What accounts for the continuing popularity of *Animal House*? The easy explanation is that male boomers who have never grown up like to relive the immature antics of their college days. But could it be something else?

Could it be that even as male boomers have aged, rather than become Alpha males, they have divided themselves into Delta males and Omega males? The Deltas became the fathers who adopted a laissez faire attitude about their kids drinking, cutting classes and otherwise having a bit too much fun. The Omega parents are typified by the guys who went ballistic when their kids wore baseball caps backwards. There is also a fence-straddling group that sometimes feels pulled by one camp, then the other.

And is it possible that the popularity of *Animal House* has been resuscitated by the long-awaited arrival of boomers in the White House? We had one boomer President of the United States who was a classic Delta: oversized libido, an occasional toke, and skilled in the artful dodging of the military draft. His impeachment trial was about as fair—and just about as useful—as the disciplinary hearing in *Animal House*, when charges were brought against the Deltas for taking liberties with their female guests.

The other boomer President started out as a Delta—even if he doesn't admit to following Bluto's sage counsel, "My advice to you is to start drinking heavily"—but his membership in the Lucky Sperm Club led to his recruitment by the Omegas. His presidency is defined by neatness, punctuality, and an abiding need to go to war.

And to those of us who continue to watch *Animal House* as we fend off solicitations to join AARP, there is just a touch of irony when we remember this: when *Animal House* begins, we naturally assume that the title refers to the raucous Deltas. But as it reaches what passes for its crescendo, after a roomful of Omegas beat up a lone Delta armed with only a bouquet of flowers, we are not so subtly informed that the militaristic bullies are the real "animal house."

46

TURN ON, TUNE IN, DROP DEAD?

In case some boomer hasn't noticed, most TV shows, movies and other forms of entertainment are created today for a certain "demographic." But it is not our free spending, hedonistic baby boom generation. For reasons I've never quite understood, most entertainment is aimed at another cohort. You may have met them. They are our children, the incomparable 18-34 year olds. To TV producers, we boomers are no longer relevant. We're not even in the parking lot of the ballpark of relevance.

In an effort to feed more new programs to the insatiable 18-34 crowd, a young whiz kid at one network has plans to "retool" old shows that were popular with boomers into more youthful fare. Here is a sneak preview:

- *Father Knows Bust.* A bunch of pathetic, 50-something men judge topless swimsuit competitions among women young enough to be their daughters.

- *Ain't Elsewhere.* In a rundown Boston neighborhood, 20-somethings dressed only in body paint compete in a spelling bee.

- *The Few Get Ill.* Young Dr. Richard Kimball and his buxom sidekick, Phillippa Gerard, travel from city to city, treating rare infections caused by body piercing.

- *Murphy Brawn.* Irish-American female weightlifters compete until they become pregnant; then *they* get lifted into the air by Dan Quayle look-alikes.

- *Happy Daze.* Ritchie, Fonz and their friends take Ecstasy. Then they take some more.

- *R*A*S*H.* Teams of college juniors and seniors with communicable skin diseases mud wrestle. The first team to show a new case of chicken pox wins.

- *The Moneymooners.* Well proportioned young men and women drop their trousers at busy downtown street corners as pedestrians and drivers toss coins into baskets.

- *NYPD Goo.* Cops round up contestants to compete in 100-meter freestyle races in the New York sewers.

- *Chill Street Blues.* Young burger flippers hang out during their break, sharing war stories.

- *Slaw & Order.* Young cops and assistant DAs compete in three-legged races through an Olympic-size pool filled with cole slaw.

- *The Man From D.R.U.N.K.L.E.* GEN-Yers Napoleon Solo and Ilya Kuryakin lead competing binge drinking teams. The first victim of alcohol poisoning gets to compete in the Brain Death Lightning Round.

If these shows don't develop a following, the network has a "Plan B." To expand its audience (however reluctantly) to attract some boomers, they plan to spin off "reality" and other shows that are popular among our kids into programs that are calculated to appeal to boomers. We've stolen a secret list of those shows, and here it is:

- *Extreme Takeover.* An Enron-like company borrows billions to make hostile takeovers of small cities. This show already has a spin-off waiting for release....

- *American Idle.* Groups of 50-something boomers in small, mid-American cities, all of whom have been out of work for at least two years, compete to write the warmest letter to President Bush thanking for him the latest tax cuts.

- *No Millionaire.* Aging boomers, whose 401(k) plans were heavily weighted to WorldCom stock, compete to see how many credit cards they can max out in a month.

- *The Hatchelor.* During the day, the senior senator from Utah and his friends on the Senate Judiciary Committee issue sound bites to the press about how Democrats have poisoned the judicial confirmation process since the Madison administration. At night, Orrin and his buddy, Ted Kennedy, carouse at DC night spots.

- *Rear Factor.* A row of sedentary boomers sits on a park bench eating high-caloric snack foods until their backsides expand enough to force the guy or gal on the end to fall off.

- *A Clear Eye For The Farsighted Guy.* Each week, a team of specialists led by an ophthalmologist examines a presbyopic boomer and recommends bifocals, trifocals or Lasik surgery.

- *Bill and Grace.* Boomer-in-chief Bill Clinton tries to seduce Princess Grace of Monaco, gets arrested and convicted, and then pardons himself.

- *Average Bo.* A one-time perfect "10," now showing her age, learns to cope in a world where she is just an average "5."

- *Reviver.* As boomers watching some of these shows go into cardiac arrest, boomer doctors armed with defibrillators shock them back to life.

Happy viewing!

47

BOND. JAMES BOND.

When the epitaph for the baby boom generation is finally written, historians will discover one character that seemed to catch our generation's imagination from the early days of the Cold War into the 21st century. He was born in print, but came to life for most of us in motion pictures. And these films continued to proliferate long after the books had been exhausted, and even as an array of different stars playing the leading role came and went.

By now, you must surely know who I am talking about. His name is Bond. James Bond.

The original James Bond books by author Ian Fleming first began to appear in about 1953. Fleming's loyal following, which included John F. Kennedy, inspired a transition of Bond to the big screen.

The first James Bond movie starring Sean Connery, *Dr. No*, was released in 1962. Like most "next big things," I missed out on this one—at least initially. But I did manage to see *Goldfinger* during the 1964-65 Christmas break my freshman year of college. I was hooked! Before returning to school for my first semester final exams, I read as many Bond novels as I could. By the time I was done, I was a fan for life. (Let's not go into the impact this had on my freshman grades.)

The rest—as they say—is history. The last few James Bond books Ian Fleming wrote were, sadly, disappointing compared with his earlier work. But this seemed to have little or no impact on the Bond movie franchise, which took on a life of its own—a life with no end in sight.

The pattern for the movies never changed. Bond would be summoned to meet with his boss "M" after the inevitable flirtation with the love-starved Miss Moneypenny. M would lay out for Bond the plot that had to be foiled, which invariably threatened at least the British Isles, if not the entire solar system. Bond would then call on "Q," the armorer who would train Bond to use the latest gadgets.

Bond would then go meet the bad guy. The first meeting was usually cordial, but the plot invariably thickened. Bond would then destroy the bad guy's weapons and infrastructure, saving humanity once again. Then, as we all exhaled and rooted for Bond to finally have some fun with his love interest, the bad guys would appear to rise again from the ashes, only to be terminated with extreme prejudice by Bond in some creative way (for example, Goldfinger being sucked out of a pressurized plane).

So what is it about James Bond that has sustained its popularity throughout the entire adult life of the baby boom generation? For starters, there are those three old standbys: sex, violence and the triumph of good over evil.

But Mr. Fleming seemed to have been somewhat prescient with regard to the changing nature of evil. During the early days of James Bond at the height of the Cold War, evil was personified by the Soviet Union. Fleming captured this tension with a keen eye in *From Russia With Love*—perhaps his very best.

But as we all know, the nature of evil changed over time. With the passing of the Evil Empire, the focus shifted to "rogue states" such as Libya and North Korea. And more recently, we have seen evil shift again to what might be called rogue non-states, such as al Qaeda.

But Ian Fleming saw this coming. Indeed, some of his scariest bad guys were wealthy freelance megalomaniacs such as Ernst Stavro Blofeld and his organization, SPECTRE. Were these villains, conceived a half-century ago, all that different from Osama bin Laden?

I thought about James Bond recently, when I channel-surfed one evening and stumbled on yet another Bond marathon on a cable channel. Coincidentally, the next day I heard that Pierce Brosnan would be making no more Bond movies. I predict that there will be at least one more Agent 007. And it's entirely possible that the next 007 will be young enough to be the son of us baby boomers or—this being the 21st century, after all—the daughter.

48

PUSHING 60 AND STILL PUZZLED

I have been a fan of crossword puzzles for a half-century. You know the type: *New York Times* puzzles only; ink only, no pencils (and certainly no erasers); pooh-poohs the easy Monday puzzles in favor of the more challenging Friday and Saturday offerings; the whole shebang.

So I find it fascinating and surprising that my crossword puzzles hobby has turned out to be one of the saving graces of impending codgerdom, at least for this baby boomer.

How so? Well, it turns out that puzzle makers seem to like to make their creations difficult by expecting solvers to know a little bit (and sometime maybe more) about a lot of different things. Either that, or they end up having to scavenge for really obscure words to make the puzzle work. Either way, that often translates into trivia from many different decades. That could make it tough for young pups who *think* they're good at solving puzzles. But for some of us boomers who are now living in our seventh different decade (count 'em!), we've been there.

To illustrate, here's a sampling of clues from *Times* puzzles over a period of a couple of months. Take a look at how it can finally pay off to be pushing 60. Let's skip the 1940s, since not even the most precocious boomers were into gathering useless information at that point. (Answers below.)

- The 1950s. 1. Old Mideast grp.; 2. Straight man of comedy; 3. Old brand advertised by Bucky Beaver; 4. Ike's opponent, twice; 5. Two-time loser to D.D.E. (*there are many variations on this one*); 6. "_____ Love" (1957 #1 hit); 7. "Put Your Head on My Shoulder" singer, 1959

- The 1960s. 8. "Java" blower; 9. 1962 expansion team; 10. "_____ la Douce," 1963 film; 11. 1964 Hitchcock film

- The 1970s. 12. "One L" author; 13. 1972 Olympic swimming sensation; 14. Negotiator at Vladivostok, 1974

- The 1980s. 15. Movie chameleon of 1983; 16. 1983 flick "_____ and the Cruisers"; 17. "Slaves of New York" author Janowitz

- Double-decade clues. 18. 1980s-90s TV drama

- The 1990s. 19. 1992 and '96 third-party candidate; 20. "Heat" co-star, 1995; 21. 1998's _____ Report

- The 2000s (or whatever moniker eventually sticks to this decade). 22. Armstrong on wheels; 23. One of the baseball Boones; 24. 2004 sword-and-sandals flick; 25. Pitcher Derek, 2004 Red Sox World Series hero; 26. 2005 portrayer of Wonka

- ANSWERS (some of which—I confess—I had to get from the next day's paper): 1. UAR; 2. ABBOTT; 3. IPANA; 4. ADLAI; 5. AES; 6. APRIL; 7. ANKA; 8. HIRT; 9. METS; 10. IRMA; 11. MARNIE; 12. TUROW; 13. MARKSPITZ; 14. FORD; 15. ZELIG; 16. EDDIE; 17. TAMA; 18. LALAW; 19. PEROT; 20. ALPACINO; 21. STARR; 22. LANCE; 23. BRET; 24. TROY; 25. LOWE; 26. DEPP

Of course, being a know-it-all usually backfires. It did for me recently when I came across the clue, "Astronaut Collins." Aha, I thought: 1969! The first moon landing! The guy who orbited the moon while the other guys, Armstrong and Aldrin, were prospecting for rocks. The answer, of course, should be MICHAEL.

But MICHAEL didn't fit in the six-letter space. If I had been paying attention to news of space travel more recently, I would not have had to wait for the answer in the next day's puzzle. And it wasn't a guy.

It was EILEEN.

Boomers I Love

49

A BOOMER I LOVE: BOB EDWARDS

There's a good chance you've never heard of Bob Edwards. If your commute is very short, or if you take a train or bus, you may not have ever crossed paths with Bob Edwards. For multiple decades of his career, I didn't know of him either.

But beginning in 2000, I began to spend an hour or more in my car each morning. Before long, in the course of surfing radio stations from music that I'm too old to appreciate, to right-wing lunacy, to commercials by car dealers screaming "Low credit? No credit? No problem!," I discovered Bob Edwards on National Public Radio's "Morning Edition."

With his deep voice, his disarming touch of irony, and his eclectic yet low-key sophistication, Bob Edwards made my morning commute—through traffic that could make a grown boomer weep—a time I could actually enjoy. His in-depth reporting, his playful interviews, and his long view of things made him my ideal car pool partner: he always kept me engaged, and I never had to reciprocate.

I didn't know much about Bob Edwards—great radio personalities, like shrinks, don't reveal much about themselves—until recently. Sadly, I came to learn about him only when the rocket scientists who run NPR decided that Bob should give up his early-morning show (for which he would rise each weekday at 1 a.m.) and become a "Senior Correspondent." And they decided that this must take place in the spring of 2004, even though Bob was just a few months away from completing his 25th year at "Morning Edition."

I joined what proved to be a mob of listeners and contributors that bombarded NPR with letters and e-mails decrying their shortsightedness. But it was to no avail. NPR's standard response made reference to the huge bequest it had received from Joan Kroc (the widow of the McDonald's founder), and insisted that change was needed. Translation: "We've got Joan's money; we don't need yours."

It turns out that Bob Edwards, whose wisdom and erudition made me think he was from the Brokaw "greatest" generation, is actually a boomer, born in 1947. He grew up in Louisville, Kentucky. He got his start in radio across the river in New Albany, Indiana, where he used to hang out at a local station. One day, a regular announcer was suddenly unavailable, and Bob got to fill in. He ultimately went on to NPR, first doing a stint on "All Things Considered," and then 24 1/2 years at "Morning Edition."

Perhaps this was just coincidence, but Bob was "relieved" of his "Morning Edition" duties just as he completed a book he had written about Edward R. Murrow. We early boomers have dim memories of Murrow on the TV show "See It Now." But before there was television, and before he almost single-handedly defanged Sen. Joseph McCarthy, Murrow earned his stripes in radio. In what was then a technological miracle, Murrow reported World War II live from Europe.

There is a certain symmetry to Bob Edwards paying tribute to Edward R. Murrow. Murrow was a giant in radio when radio was the only source for immediate news. His accomplishments demonstrated the great power of the medium at a time of that medium's greatest influence.

On the other hand, Bob Edwards entered radio at a time when it risked being shoved aside by television. The conventional wisdom was simple: who needs a medium that is merely audio when TV provides both audio and video?

Bob Edwards helped answer that question. He provided radio programming in which the conversation and commentary was so engrossing that pictures would be just a distraction. He helped radio not only survive the advent of TV (and later the Internet), but thrive. And on the most basic and personal level, he was good company to those of us fighting traffic who can't read a newspaper, can't watch TV, but crave the kind of soft-spoken sanity that Bob Edwards provided.

So here's to one wonderful boomer. Bob, enjoy life after "Morning Edition." Catch up on your sleep if you can. And just know that lots of us hope we keep hearing your wonderful voice—and the wonderful content it conveys—for years to come.

50

A BOOMER I LOVE: SCOTT TUROW

For those who like to criticize baby boomers, there are certain "types" of boomers that critics like to single out. A particular favorite is the boomer who is smart, but thinks he's *really* smart; who thinks he's more talented than the rest of us; and who thinks people should care about what he or she has to say.

For this reason, at first glance, Scott Turow might seem to be the type of boomer everyone should love to hate. But it turns out he *is* really smart. It also turns out he is a *very* talented novelist; for my money, his books are not just the best of their genre, they're among the best in *any* genre. And in recent years, it has turned out that we should care a great deal about what Scott Turow has to say, particularly on the subject of capital punishment.

Scott Turow (boomer class of 1949) grew up in Chicago and was bright enough to go to Amherst College. He then studied (and later taught) creative writing at Stanford. He then went on to Harvard Law School. But while so many Harvard Law grads put in their three years, get their ticket punched, and move on to Wall Street firms, Turow chose to write about his law school experience. His first book, *One L* (1977), became a classic study of the often bizarre methods used to train lawyers.

Turow returned to Chicago and worked as an Assistant U.S. Attorney for several years. He then moved on to private practice at a prominent firm. To all appearances, he seemed destined to become just another successful big-firm, big-city, big-income lawyer.

But somewhere inside Turow, some sort of chemical reaction was taking place between his early training in creative writing and his later work as a lawyer. Much of the chemistry played out on the commuter trains he rode to and from work in downtown Chicago. The result was his first novel, *Presumed Innocent* (1987), a bestseller that propelled him straight to the top of the lawyer-writes-about-lawyer genre.

Turow went on to write a string of first-rate novels, all revolving around Kindle County, a Midwestern city Turow created to house his characters, who sometimes straddle more than one of his books. My favorite (if not that of the critics) was *The Laws Of Our Fathers* (1996), a haunting look back at how the actions of campus radicals in the 1960s planted the seeds of a brutal murder in Kindle County decades later. It is a story that only a boomer could tell.

By the time he turned 50, Turow could have rested on his laurels (and his royalties). But in 2000, the capital punishment system in his native Illinois was itself going through a death rattle. As a result of DNA testing and aggressive advocacy, it turned out that almost half the inmates on Illinois' death row were not even guilty. The governor declared a moratorium on executions and appointed Turow to a blue-ribbon commission to see if the system could be fixed.

Turow says he approached the task as an "agnostic" with no preconceived views about whether the death penalty was right or wrong. He seems to have truly approached the subject with an open mind, in contrast to those with fixed and largely emotional views at both ends of the spectrum. His willingness to listen and learn led him to some fresh and valuable insights into the subject of the death penalty, which he has shared in books, articles and talks. If there ever comes a time when American society figures out the right answer to the capital punishment question, Scott Turow will stand out as someone who really helped make it happen.

So we boomers can thank Scott Turow for spoiling the stereotype about how everyone in our generation thinks he or she is so smart and so important. Sure, lots of us do fill that bill. But Scott Turow is one smart guy who has put his bountiful talents to good use. He has not only given us a shelf full of wonderful reads. He has actually made thoughtful contributions to public discourse at a time when no one seems to listen to anyone else.

51

A BOOMER I LOVE: RON HOWARD

There is no shortage of baby boomers who have reached the heights in the entertainment field. For example, our generation includes great performers like Meryl Streep (born 1949) and great directors like Stephen Spielberg (born 1946).

But is there a boomer in show business whose work has really *defined* our generation? Is there someone who has been out there during every phrase of our lives, and who has grown in stature as our generation has aged? Someone whose work is intimately related to the boomer generation?

You may be able to come up with a candidate or two who might be better than mine. But for my money, you could do a heck of a lot worse than Ron Howard.

Howard isn't quite as old as some of us boomers, having been born in Oklahoma in 1954. But he is a boomer through and through. And he has entertained our generation and others for four decades, growing from an adorable child actor into directing giant.

Of course, we all remember his first role as Opie Taylor on *The Andy Griffith Show* (1960-68). In Mayberry, a town full of kind and innocent people, Opie was the sweetest of them all. During a period of assassinations, war and turmoil beyond belief, Howard and the grown-ups on the show gave us a chance to step back into the innocent, rural 1950s for a half hour each week.

After a few years of diminished visibility, Howard returned to TV as Richie Cunningham in *Happy Days* (1974-80). With the convulsions of Vietnam and Watergate behind us, the country craved another stint of still-innocent, small-town America. Richie, the Fonz and the rest provided it to us with a weekly serving of comfort.

Like many others, Howard outgrew the small screen. He starred in *American Graffiti* in 1973, and appeared in *The Shootist* in 1976, earning a Golden Globe nomination. Having crossed the line into movies, Howard never looked back. And along the way he also made the transition from the front of the camera to the back.

Howard made a number of popular movies, such as *Parenthood* (1989) and *Apollo 13* (1995), directing stars like Steven Martin and Tom Hanks. But my personal favorite Howard film—until recently, that is—was *Backdraft* (1991), which explored the lives of firefighters who have to deal with crackpot arsonists while dealing with sibling rivalry and fighting their other personal inner demons.

Those of us who thought Howard had peaked discovered not long ago that we were badly mistaken. His 2001 film, *A Beautiful Mind*, starring Russell Crowe, won the Academy Award for Best Picture, and won Howard the award for Best Director, both of which were richly deserved. The story about Princeton mathematician John Nash who rises as a Cold War cryptographer, only to descend into horrific mental illness, is guaranteed to haunt every viewer who is fortunate enough to see the film.

In a sense, Howard's work has touched on and captured so many aspects of the second half of the 20th Century—the boomer era, such as (in roughly chronological order) the Cold War (*A Beautiful Mind*), the innocence of the Eisenhower era and its aftermath (*The Andy Griffith Show*, *Happy Days* and *American Graffiti*), the space race (*Apollo 13*), and the sea change in family relationships that has pervaded our entire lifetimes (*Parenthood*). And how's this for a boomer credential: in 1971, he was a contestant on *The Dating Game*. (He chose Bachelorette #2.)

The baby boom generation is sometimes accused of destroying what some politicians and pundits call "family values." Not Ron Howard. He is said to have cast his parents, his brother and his daughter in small roles, and he has been married to his high school sweetheart since 1975. (He has a habit of naming his children after the place they were conceived, but—hey—no one's perfect.)

And here's what may be the best part of all. Howard is just now in his early 50s, a time when doing whatever you do finally seems easier. Howard's best work may still be coming.

Stay tuned.

52

A BOOMER I LOVE: CAL RIPKEN, JR.

What did *you* do from 1982 through 1998?

If you're a typical baby boomer, chances are you spent much of that time married to a spouse, or maybe two, and raised some kids. You probably had a couple of different jobs, or maybe even more, or maybe you owned a business. If you're lucky, you earned a living for all those years. And, if you're like most of us, you probably did some C work, some B work, and maybe even some A work.

But did you show up for work, at the same company, *every single day*, over a seventeen-year period?

The boomer we honor here, Cal Ripken, Jr., did precisely that. Ripken is younger than the first wave of boomers, born in 1960 when many of us were already approaching adolescence. But I for one am proud that he's officially a boomer.

Ripken played in 2,632 consecutive baseball games for the Baltimore Orioles, breaking Lou Gehrig's previous record by some three years and 500 games. For one five-year period, Ripken didn't even miss an *inning*. Because Ripken spent much time on the disabled list after 1998, for all intents and purposes, Ripken never missed a game for his entire major league career.

Baseball is not as physically punishing as football, hockey or even basketball. And a five-month winter break (more if you don't make the playoffs) can heal a lot of wounds. But when you play offense in baseball, balls are hurled in your direction at close to 100 mph; and when you play defense in the infield, as Ripken did, line drives can come screaming at you even faster. Ripken suffered the occasional back spasm, twisted knee, sprained ankle and even a broken nose, but he sucked them up much like he sucked up ground balls hit to the left side of the infield.

Staying healthy is one thing; but in baseball, to stay in the lineup day after day, you have to deliver day after day. And Ripken did. His fielding earned him two Gold Glove awards; he set the career record for his Orioles, for hits, runs, home runs and numerous other offensive categories; and his overall play made him Rookie of the Year in 1982 and, later, the American League's Most Valuable Player—twice. In 2007, he was handily voted into the Baseball Hall of Fame.

Ripken could have taken the occasional break, particularly as he inched toward elder statesmanship, a stage that one reaches far too quickly in the sports world. There are often games at the end of the season that no longer affect the teams' standings, and veteran players sometimes sit one out and let a younger player fill in. Maybe some veterans do, but not Cal Ripken.

The vast majority of us boomers toil away in fields a lot less glamorous than baseball. But the pressures we face aren't all that different. Take the issue of staying healthy. Sure, there are lots of boomers who call in sick, for legitimate reasons, and others take regularly scheduled "mental health days" and manage to use up every allotted sick day each year. But I know plenty of boomers who seem never to be out sick. Like Cal Ripken, they show up at the office nursing a bad back, or popping aspirin to fight a low-grade fever. But they *always* show up.

Staying valuable enough to remain in the "starting lineup" every day is something else altogether. We all know a few people who coast through life on inborn talent. But most of us have to do it the hard way, putting in extra time and going the second or even the third mile. Yes, there are many talented, hardworking boomers who lose their jobs through forces beyond their control, like mass layoffs. But the Cal Ripkens among them are often the ones who bounce back most quickly, even if they have to step back into the "minor leagues" for a spell. You just know they'll be back in the big leagues, sooner or later.

Woody Allen is believed to have once said, "Ninety percent of life is just showing up." The Cal Ripkens we all know, in all walks of life, suggest that maybe Woody's number is just a tad low.

The Next Generation (Finally!)

53

TEACH YOUR PARENTS WELL

"I'm sorry, we need someone with more and broader experience—someone more savvy and versatile—someone who knows all the little tricks and angles. You know—someone about half your age."

This conversation is, of course, imaginary, but only because human resources people today are more subtle and more politically correct. The subject of this conversation, of course, is sophistication with computers and the rest of modern technology. Something that barely existed when we boomers started our careers, but which now permeates virtually every business and every walk of life. Something that our own kids and their contemporaries know one heck of a lot more about than most of us.

Is the baby boom generation—which has spent a half a century thinking it is so damned smart—being humiliated and left in the dust by the next generation? When our kids talk about how dumb and pathetic their parents are, as all kids have spoken about all parents for all time, are our kids actually going to be *right*?

If so, we're not in bad company. We're not the first generation to be left behind by our kids, and we surely won't be the last.

Think, for a moment, about the immigrants who came to the United States in the early 20th Century to become first-generation Americans. While the immigrant parents worked, their children learned English—perhaps the first in their families to learn a new language in hundreds of years. Imagine the feeling of liberation this brought: the ability to read signs, newspapers and books, to go to college, and to live the American dream. And all the while, their tired old monolingual parents could only watch from the sidelines.

Or consider our own parents, some of whom were the first in their families to own and drive cars. What freedom! Imagine how our grandparents felt, watching their kids travel wherever and whenever they wanted, without schedules, without tickets or subway tokens (in those days, without even seatbelts!), and with just a couple of bucks to buy a tank of gas. With cars, they could flee the teeming cities and move to the suburbs. But most of our grandparents had to be content to sit (literally and figuratively) in the back seat—that is, with us.

But what about *our* generation? Sure, we always thought we could do so much more than our parents. But compared with the cataclysmic changes that occurred during earlier generations, was anything new that we did really such a big deal?

Yes, we had television. But all you had to do was watch it. And we did: we watched cops from the first Joe Friday to Andy Sipowicz; we watched doctors from Ben Casey to Mark Green; we watched lawyers from Perry Mason to Alan Shore. But our parents watched too.

Were we pioneers in air travel? No way. We weren't the first, and all we had to do was board the planes (with or without nail clippers) and just sit there. Fast food? All we did was eat it—lots of it. No big achievement there.

Yes, we learned to use the new technologies of our day: stereo systems, touch-tone phones, color TV and, later, VCRs. But these were incremental improvements, not life altering milestones. And, besides, all we really did was push a lot of buttons.

Some of us actually got a taste of computers back in the dark ages of the '60s. I actually took a college course in programming those monster IBM machines, punching cards and waiting two or three days for my programs to be run, only to then forget about computers for about 20 years. Did this help prepare me for the modern computer revolution? Hardly; if anything, that foregone opportunity only heightens my embarrassment over my current lack of computer sophistication.

And so it seems that we boomers will have to sit back and take our licks while younger generations intimidate us with internet this, e-mail that and wireless everything. As Crosby, Stills, Nash & Young might say today, "Teach your *parents* well."

54

YOUNG WHIPPERSNAPPERS

With the 2008 presidential campaign ready to begin in earnest, let's briefly look back just one short election cycle. The group that ran for the 2004 Democratic presidential nomination was described in many ways by members of the chattering classes, with the description usually depending on the political proclivities of the person doing the analysis. (Too liberal! Republicans in sheep's clothing! Can't beat Bush!) But there was one description that commentators of all stripes could get behind: another (yawn) bunch of boomers and almost-boomers. Indeed, the sheer size of the pack seemed to be a reflection of our super-sized generation.

A few of the 2004 Democratic wannabes (including Dennis Kucinich, Carol Moseley-Braun and early frontrunner Howard Dean)—remember them?—were early boomers, born in the late 1940s. A couple (John Edwards and the Rev. Al Sharpton) were born in the early 1950s, but they are still true boomers. Four other candidates were not technically boomers, but they were close, born during World War II (John Kerry, Dick Gephardt, Joe Lieberman and Wesley Clark). The only candidate of the original ten who was clearly of another generation was the first one to drop out: Bob Graham (born 1936). Even the most talked-about non-candidate, Hillary Clinton (born 1947), is a boomer. Since President Bush (born 1946) is, of course, a boomer as well, it was a virtual certainty that the winner of the 2004 election would be a member (or an almost-member) of our postwar generation.

But it didn't necessarily have to turn out this way. Under the U.S. Constitution, you only have to be 35 to be elected president. What does that mean? Well, it means that in 2004, to be old enough to run, you must have been born in 1969 or earlier.

So who are we talking about here? Well, the group that was old enough to run for president in 2004 includes the likes of Anne Heche, Sean "Puffy" Combs, Halle Berry, Vin Diesel, Ken Griffey, Jr., and the entire cast of "Friends."

A boomer held on to the White House in 2004, but what about 2008? By then, boomers will have occupied the Oval Office for 16 years—pretty close to a whole generation—and we may start hearing talk about the torch being passed to another new generation. And who might that include? Do the math: anyone born in 1973 or earlier, such as Ben Affleck, Cameron Diaz, Winona Ryder, and Jorge Posada.

Sooner or later, boomers are going to have to deal with the unthinkable: a post-boomer running the country. Think of all the hand wringing! I can just hear the bellyaching by our huge generation when it finally faces the prospect of being over the hill. Imagine lines like this being hurled at TV sets during presidential debates between such young whippersnappers:

- When you were in diapers, we were on the front lines campaigning for Clean Gene McCarthy and protesting the Vietnam war. (Or maybe we were just high on grass or beer—oddly enough, we can't remember which.)

- When you were in junior high, we were helping to build the "Me Generation," elevating greed and apathy to heights never before seen.

- When you were in high school, we boomers were starting families and having kids with adorable names. Why, if it wasn't for us, we wouldn't now be seeing wedding announcements like "Jennifer Jessica Jones marries Jason Jared Johnson today on the uptown platform of the Jay Street subway station. Judge Judy will perform the ceremony."

- When you were still in college, we were enriching the lives of our kids, dragging them to so many school and after-school activities, lessons, games, leagues and programs that our kids were too tired to go to college, so they retired to Florida instead.

- And when you were fooling around with recreational drugs like Ecstasy, we were taking *real* drugs for *serious* problems, like ROGAINE, BOTOX and VIAGRA.

No, it won't be a pretty picture. But the generations which are following ours into the White House and other positions of authority will no doubt find the right words to get us off their case. They will dismiss us with something like "Get over it," or maybe "Get a life." Or perhaps they will hit us with my personal favorite:

"Suck it up."

55

SO'S YOUR OLD MAN

One interesting by-product of the baby boom generation approaching geezerdom is that in the case of a number of celebrities and other boldfaced names, we can vividly remember and wax eloquently about their equally (or more, or less) notable parents. The most obvious example is President George W. Bush, whose father was already a significant political player back when we were young. But there are lots of other multigenerational political families, such as the Bayhs of Indiana: Birch, who served in the Senate from 1963 to 1981, and his son Evan, a Senator since 1999. Or take the two Richard Daleys, who collectively served as Mayor of Chicago for most of the last 50 years.

We see this phenomenon in other areas, like entertainment. When we watch current performers like Jamie Lee Curtis, Emilio Esteves, Mariska Hargitay or Kate Hudson, we can bore our kids to tears by comparing them—for better or worse—with their well-known parents (Janet Leigh, Martin Sheen, Jayne Mansfield and Goldie Hawn).

In politics and show business, it is often possible to stay in the limelight for several decades. For that reason, we sometimes see generations overlap, as they did when both Martin Sheen and his other son Charlie appeared in *Wall Street*. Ben Stiller's career got rolling while his father Jerry played George's wacky father Frank Costanza on *Seinfeld*. Or, in politics, we have Patrick Kennedy serving in the House since 1994, while his father Ted has been in the Senate since yours truly was a sophomore in high school.

But there is one area where generational overlap is rare, because the half-life of one's career is so short: sports, where you can probably count on one good decade, maybe part of another, and then the reflexes slow down, the muscles soften, and you're toast.

Perhaps one reason why sports fans of the boomer persuasion seem to delight in watching the athletic exploits of those whose parents delighted us years ago is that those parents were in their prime during the "heyday" of sports, which is to say any time our kids are too young to remember. Take the case of baseball player Barry Bonds. Well before he was accused of using steroids, he seemed poised to pass the larger-than-life Babe Ruth in career home runs, and maybe even break the record set by Hank Aaron, who in turn passed the Babe some 30 years ago. But boomers who followed baseball around the 1970s can't resist comparing Barry to his father, Bobby Bonds. Bobby never took a run at the Babe's record, but he was one heck of an exciting player, hitting over 300 home runs and stealing 461 bases.

Barry Bonds is perhaps today's most notable example of an athlete who has followed in a parent's footsteps. But there are plenty of others, such as the Mannings of football, the Waltons of basketball, and the Fraziers of boxing (Joe and his *daughter*).

Some great athletes have shown that they can give us thrills for more than one generation. You might say those good jock genes are the gift that keeps on giving.

But are we about to enter a phase that once would have seemed unthinkable? Might we be getting close to a time where the *grandchildren* of the athletes we admired as kids move into prominence?

We can already see it in NASCAR racing, where careers can last longer than in other sports, and where Richard Petty has been followed by his son *and* his grandson. But what about other sports, where careers are usually shorter?

Let's do the math. Many of us started following sports seriously as early adolescents. The big stars in those days were perhaps about 30 years old, born around 1930. Let's assume those folks had kids around 1955, and that *those* kids had their own kids around 1980. If any of those kids are heading toward big-time sports success, it could start to happen right about—*now*.

If so, we are entering uncharted waters. We may soon be able to sit in the ballpark and cry out to the visiting team's star, "You're a bum, so's your old man, and so was *his* old man!"

56

THE CRYSTAL BALL

Just recently, I heard a discussion on radio involving a young man from an organization called "No Kidding" deciding in his early 20s that he never wanted to have children and was therefore having a vasectomy. What impressed me wasn't the substance of his views. It was how sure he was that he would adhere to these views for the rest of his life—perhaps another 50 or so years.

Allow this budding codger from the boomer generation this observation. The younger you are when you make life-altering decisions, the harder it is to predict that the choice will play out well over time. Let's consider something less emotional than childrearing, such as career selection. For many boomers, when we went to college, we chose a major that would help us start out in the careers we then envisioned for ourselves. But let's get real here: at the age of 18, we were trying to predict what we'd like to be doing in our 20s, our 30s, and beyond. And the amount of real world insight that figured into those careers choices was pretty close to zero.

And so it is not at all remarkable that some young people who are out of college, and who have perhaps tried out one job or graduate school, decide that they need to shift gears. Some of their parents (boomers and otherwise) may object, but they are fighting a losing battle. A change at that point is a *good* thing, mostly because it is more likely to be the right choice—much more likely, in my view—than the choice made back at the age of 18. Part of it is just the inevitable result of spending a few more years in the real world. You get to see what your peers are doing and whether your bosses are still enjoying it. And you acquire what is sometimes called "negative" information: that is, insights about your initial choice and why it *doesn't* work for you. So if you learn, for example, that you *don't* like spending eight hours a day in a cubicle in front of a computer screen, you will hopefully avoid that particular problem with your next choice of careers.

Consider how this theory applies to the choice of a spouse or other partner. It's been said that people who get married at very young ages are at a high risk of ending up divorced. What a surprise!!! When you're barely out of puberty, the chances of deciding correctly that some person will remain just right for you years later are slim indeed. But once you get a little older, and have had a few relationships, your crystal ball gets a lot clearer, and you have a better idea what will work and what will drive you berserk.

So listening to this young man from "No Kidding" got me to thinking about those of us boomers who are in our late 50s. We are still making choices: whether to change jobs; whether to divorce and/or remarry; whether to retire and, if so, where; and so forth. But now we are making these decisions with a half century of experience, a record that will have included some good moves, some great moves, and some spectacular screw-ups.

So the good news is that we have a really good shot now at getting it right—or at least you'd think so. But let's not drown in a sea of hubris here. The bad news is that some of the mistakes we made—the kind of mistakes we'd like to not repeat—took place so long ago that they have slipped out of our failing memories.

And there's one more thing to keep in mind about the choices we make at this stage in life. Unlike the young man from "No Kidding" who feels he knows what he'll want 50 years from now, our horizon is a tad shorter. We only have to predict that these choices will still make sense for a decade or two or three. So if you're thinking of doing something really crazy—and I don't mean ordering coffee with caffeine—you've earned this bit of advice for someone your age:

Go for it!

978-0-595-42540-2
0-595-42540-2

www.ingramcontent.com/pod-product-compliance
Lightning Source LLC
Chambersburg PA
CBHW020436290526
45785CB00002B/882